MONEY MATTERS

Helping people with learning difficulties have more control over their money

Catherine Bewley

Values Into Action
1997

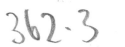

MONEY MATTERS

Copyright © 1997
Values Into Action
London

Written by
Catherine Bewley

Published in 1997 by
Values Into Action
Oxford House
Derbyshire Street
London E2 6HG
Tel: 0171 729 5436
Fax: 0171 729 7797

Registered Charity Number 1057249
A Company Limited by Guarantee
Registered in England Number 3229730

Distribution: Further copies of Money Matters can be obtained from the publisher Values Into Action.

ISBN 0 903945 41 X

Cover design:
ArtZone Co-op Ltd.
10 Back Church Lane, London E1 1LX
Tel: 0171 481 9053

DTP by
Andrew Holman

Printed by
PBS printing
100 Haltwhistle Rd
South Woodham Ferrers
CM3 5ZF
Tel: 01245 325449

Publishers statement: Throughout the preparation of this report the publishers have made every effort to ensure that the information, credits and acknowledgements given at the time of going to press, is correct. We therefore do not accept any liability for omissions or errors.

INFORMATION FOR PEOPLE WITH LEARNING DIFFICULTIES

This report is for people who work in services, people who support you and your family. Some of the things in this report are quite difficult. We want to get people to change how they manage your money, so that you can have more control over your own money. This report is to help them do this.

But there is something that is easier to understand. We have made an audio-tape for people with learning difficulties. It is called 'It's My Money!'.

This tape will tell you a lot of things about money and what to do if you are unhappy about your money.

The tape has two sides.

Side One:
* Hello! Introducing the tape.
* Learning about money.
* Jobs.
* Banks.

Side Two:
* People who need a lot of support.
* Rights.
* The end!

The tape was made by the Wigan and Leigh Free Speech Self Advocacy Group and Values Into Action.

There is a small booklet which you get with the tape. The booklet tells you more about money in words and pictures.

The tape costs £3.00

You can buy the tape by telephoning Values Into Action or get someone to telephone for you. The address is:
Values Into Action, Oxford House, Derbyshire Street, London E2 6HG
Tel: 0171 - 729 5436

Note

In order to preserve confidentiality, some of the names of people mentioned in this report have been changed.

The term 'people with learning difficulties' has been used in this report in preference to 'people with learning disabilities', an intellectual impairment' or 'mental handicap', because it is the term which people who have to live with the label say they prefer.

NATIONAL
LOTTERY
CHARITIES
BOARD

The VIA 'Unnecessary Poverty Project' was funded by the National Lottery Charities Board.

ACKNOWLEDGEMENTS

There are many people that I wish to acknowledge and thank for their invaluable involvement in the writing of this report and the research upon which it is based.

Many thanks to all the un-named practitioners, supporters, organisations, families, voluntary groups, employment agencies, advocates and workshop participants who gave generously of their time, knowledge, experience and networks. Many were very honest about the difficulties around dealing with people's money and the real dilemmas they face greatly enriched the discussion in this report. Thanks also to Denzil Lush, Master of the Court of Protection, officers at the DSS in Newcastle-upon-Tyne and national voluntary and advice agencies who offered information and discussion about issues at a national level.

I am particularly grateful to Penny Letts of the Law Society and Alison Short, VIA committee member and manager at Oxfordshire Health Trust, for detailed and extremely valuable reviewing of a draft of this report.

This research would not have been possible without the encouragement and help of colleagues at Values Into Action. Particular thanks to Jean Collins and Andrew Holman for support throughout the research and for reviewing the draft of the report, and to Yve Amor for efficient practical support.

Most importantly I am deeply grateful to all the people with learning difficulties who shared their views and experiences with me and to whom I hope I have done justice in this report. It was a wonderfully enjoyable and moving privilege to meet so many people as part of this research.

In particular, I must single out Wigan and Leigh Free Speech Self Advocacy Group whom I have known for some years now and who were involved in this project over many months. It was really fun to work with Free Speech, they shared enthusiastically in everything, including my attempts at drama! Five members of the group worked especially hard to produce the tape for people with learning difficulties which goes with this report ('It's My Money!') and so a special, personal thanks goes to Susan and James Ashurst, Brian Jones, John Francis and Paul Stirrup. My thanks also to Bridget Whittell, advisor to Free Speech, who facilitated my contact with the group and who was especially supportive in the recording studio.

Personal thanks to Angela, Jane and Louise for putting up with me during the year, especially during the writing of this report.

CONTENTS

PREFACE

REAL MONEY, REAL LIVES

This is a personal introduction to this report. During the course of this project, I ran a workshop for the Norah Fry Research Centre about people with learning difficulties and their money. Over fifty people came to the workshop, at least half being people with learning difficulties. People came from day centres and group homes, housing associations and advocacy groups, research institutions and service organisations. Some travelled all the way from Gloucester to Bristol for the hour and a half session. Money matters. Money is important and people are interested in talking about it.

However, from looking at existing research or service textbooks related to people with learning difficulties, there appears to be little guidance for staff about how to deal with personal money issues. Are personal money matters (as opposed to financial assessment) an integral part of all professional courses, staff induction and on-going training courses? Have most service organisations addressed money matters in relation to people with learning difficulties? Perhaps only in terms of developing security procedures and risk management procedures. Staff of housing and service organisations often feel unsure about dealing with people's personal money and the surrounding legal minefield. Many did not expect to have to deal with money matters when they chose their careers but it is increasingly part of professional practice. Working with people with learning difficulties and their families around money opens a Pandora's box of problems and possibilities about which many staff feel uninformed and unsupported.

Money is a complicated topic. In Bristol I found it a challenge to present a short workshop which would be interesting, useful and intelligible for the whole range of participants. Laws, benefits, the Court of Protection, banking, trust funds, procedures to protect and procedures to encourage freedom, mediating between all the vested interests, all the parties, the way money is used to control people, and the fact that money is a commodity of power in society. Understanding all of this is not easy and there have been few specific publications to help staff deal with personal finance issues.

But I also said that money is simple. There are still many, many people with learning difficulties for whom money means the £1 you have in your pocket. When I asked someone in this situation what he would change about his money if he could he said "What I would really like is £2". This man might not understand a lot of complex issues around money but access to the money he did have, even if that was £1, was incredibly important to him. When we start supporting people with learning difficulties about their money, we have to go right back to the lives they have come to expect. We can not assume that people have had any opportunities to really experience or appreciate money, learn about what it means and how it works. When we start changing people's money situation we help to change their whole lives. This is why it is so important, and so essential that organisations and staff in particular really think about how people with learning difficulties can be enabled to have much more access to and control of their own money.

Many people with learning difficulties have a lot to say about their money. During the course of this research I met people with learning difficulties from advocacy groups, day centres, education classes, group homes, residential homes, employment agencies, people who lived by themselves and those who lived with their families. Some people were organised into groups, some had specifically chosen to talk to me. Others were just around when I visited. Some people were articulate and confident in sharing their views, others were shy and unsure. Some had very little understanding of money and some people did not use speech. But everyone had something to communicate in one way or another about money. Money is an important part of life for all of us.

People with learning difficulties were keen to take part in this research. With support and encouragement, people wanted to share their views and experiences. Many were also aware of the experiences of their friends and shared their stories too. I was not just looking for bad stories; I wanted to hear about what was good, too. But I was surprised at the level of bad experiences people told me about. I did not have to dig at, or highlight, these stories; they were there on the surface.

The stories told by people with learning difficulties, their friends and supporters are threaded throughout this report. There are also a handful of experiences which serve as key examples of good and bad experiences. These life stories are described here and at various points in the following chapters. Before we start the complicated discussion about money in the following chapters, here are some people's stories to remind us of the reality of many people's experience.

Dorothy's Story

Dorothy is 54 and has lived all her life in a small village, apart from childhood years spent in a special school. At the moment she lives with her mother and stepfather and her sister lives nearby. Dorothy has cerebral palsy which makes it difficult for her to get around by herself and sometimes makes it difficult for people to know what she's saying, especially if they don't bother to listen very well. Immediately you start listening to Dorothy, it is very clear that she knows all about money and how she wants to organise it. Dorothy's frustration is that other people take all this control away from her, using her cerebral palsy as an excuse. Dorothy's mother collects her benefits from the local post office, without any involvement from Dorothy. The family has a car, paid for with Dorothy's mobility money, but do not use it for her benefit. In fact, Dorothy has to wait for the council minibus to pick her up when she needs to go somewhere.

Dorothy's mother gives her £16 a week and puts £3 in a Christmas savings club. Dorothy has never been told how much more money is claimed in her name. There was an argument about the Christmas club money: Dorothy's family threatened to take the money away, but it is a lifeline for Dorothy because she chooses to use it to pay for two weeks respite care every year, her only chance to get away from her family.

Dorothy desperately wants to move out of her family's house and into her own place. She'd really like to live in the village, sharing with a friend, but there is a long wait for suitably accessible accommodation to become available. The local council has run out of money to build or adapt properties and it is difficult finding something suitable in a fairly isolated rural area.

In the meantime, Dorothy gets more and more frustrated. She goes to a local day centre and has a personal assistant. Over the last five years her assistant and the day centre staff have really helped her decide what she wants in her life. She wants to live independently and she wants her own money. She wants to pay her own bills. So, while she is waiting for the house, the staff at the day centre have been working with Dorothy to get her a bank account, then at least she can start controlling her own money. They went to all the banks in the village and met the bank managers. Dorothy can't write and she can't get to the bank by herself but these factors were not obstacles. They negotiated with one bank which was happy for Dorothy to open an account, even agreeing that she could use a fingerprint as a signature and that she could use a room at the bank to do her transactions in privacy.

But Dorothy's family were against opening the bank account, especially her stepfather, who could see the family's control over Dorothy's money slipping away. Although her parents couldn't actually stop Dorothy opening the account, Dorothy and her supporters were worried because they believed that she would suffer serious emotional abuse if she went against her stepfather. Within weekday hours, staff could protect her, but outside these times Dorothy felt too vulnerable, especially because she lives with her family and relies on physical help from them. Dorothy's sister opened an account in her own name, saying that it would be for Dorothy if she was so concerned about having her own account. Of course, this completely misses the point that an account in someone else's name does not belong to Dorothy.

So the bank account did not get opened and Dorothy still waits for her own house. Meeting Dorothy, one is struck by her absolute clarity about what she wants and her understanding of her money situation. One is also struck by the desperation and frustration she feels, her feeling of being trapped by her situation. She knows that if she was born today she might have the chance for a different life. She knows it has taken her until now, as a person in her 50s, to see the possibility of her dreams coming true. Dorothy is someone whose eyes have been opened to the possibilities around her but who is not being allowed to meet any of her dreams. Neither she, nor the staff around her, know what to do next except wait.

Michael's Story

Michael comes from another rural family, a family of wealthy farmers. Over the years, Michael's family have not wanted much to do with him. Eventually he was able to move out of the family home, get his own place and open a bank account. Support from the social services was reduced and Michael got on with his life.

Michael received some money from his family; along with his brothers and sisters he was part owner of the family's farms. He managed his own money successfully. Michael was well known in his local village; he liked living there. People knew him and he had quite a few friends.

However, one of the 'friends' began to get money out of Michael, it seems by offering to do bits of work on his house and garden and suggesting Michael give him some money towards his efforts or pay for materials which were never actually bought. Over a number of years, £15,000 was stolen from Michael in this way.

Eventually, the fraud came to light and the person concerned was prosecuted. But the consequences for Michael were much more serious than the loss of the money. His faith in the local community was destroyed, as was his confidence in himself. At the time, no one supported him through this experience, helped him learn from it and rebuild his confidence. Instead, the response was to take the control of his money away from him, which made him feel even more of a failure. His family, to protect their money, removed him from being part owner of the family's inheritance and applied to become appointee for his benefits and receiver for his assets. Although Michael still does not have much contact with his family, he nevertheless has to ask them for money. It usually takes weeks before he receives it.

Michael is now supported by social services, who are finding it extremely difficult to get the family to say what money Michael has. It is very difficult for them to help Michael know what his financial options are without this information. For Michael, his confidence has been so reduced that he now wants to move into residential accommodation.

Josie's Story

Josie lived for many years with her father. They were very close but eventually they agreed it would be good for her to live more independently, especially as her father was getting older. Josie moved into a shared house owned by a housing association. Although it was officially called a residential home, in fact Josie didn't need that much support. She was able to get on with her life, which included looking after her own money. She kept her own benefit books, cashed them and paid the necessary bills. She also had a bank account which she accessed herself, again managing her own bank books. Josie really liked living in the home and staff positively encouraged her to manage her own money.

Josie's close relationship with her father continued over the years. He was also very supportive of her managing her own money. Eventually, however, he died, leaving her a few thousand pounds which went into her bank account.

Unbeknown to Josie, her father's brother was not happy that this money had gone to Josie. Josie had had little contact with her uncle for many years. Nevertheless, he applied to the Court of Protection to become her receiver, which would give him control over her money. Current procedures and the volume of work at the Court of Protection mean that applications involving only small amounts of money are simply checked for procedural errors but there is no direct contact with the applicant or the subject. The Court of Protection requires only that a supporting form is completed by a doctor who vouches that the individual is not capable of looking after their own money (see Chapter 2 for a further discussion of the Court of Protection). In Josie's case, her uncle's application was supported by a doctor who was a close friend of his, someone who had only met Josie once but who was prepared to say that because she had learning difficulties she was not able to manage her own money.

The first Josie knew about this whole process was a letter which arrived informing her that she now had a receiver who controlled her money and that she would have to apply to the Court, via the receiver, to get any of it, despite the fact that this is her money and she had been managing it by herself for years. Josie no longer has direct access to her benefits or her bank account or the money left to her by her father. Staff were very concerned about this situation but did not know what to do about it.

Alan and Tom's Story

Alan and Tom both lived for many years in a long stay hospital situated on the outskirts of a town. As plans for the closure of the hospital developed, most people moved out into group homes belonging to a local housing association. Alan and Tom moved out about two years ago, both of them relieved to see the back of the hospital. They looked forward to starting a new life in a new home, based in an ordinary town, doing ordinary things. For both men, this also meant being able to receive their own benefits and open local bank accounts.

But, unknown to them, their cases were referred to the Court of Protection, along with those of most people being resettled from hospitals in the area. While the Court of Protection works its way through this pile of applications, the assets of ex-patients are frozen. Their benefits are sent to the housing association but the money they have in the hospital bank has not been released. Every week, Alan and Tom have to make the long bus journey back to the place they never wanted to set eyes on again to get money from the hospital bank. This has been going on for two years. Apart from being expensive and time consuming for them, and apart from the fact that it prevents them properly settling in their new homes and opening local bank accounts, it also causes great distress to the men, who have to walk back up the long drive and enter a place they hate and fear.

Fiona's Story

Fiona left school just a few years ago and now attends classes at an independent adult education college. Fiona is young and enthusiastic; she has dreams for her life; she has things she wants to achieve. Fiona lives in housing association property and has her own post office book and benefit books. She gets incapacity benefit.

Fiona was able to get work in the college's nursery. They paid her £15 a week, the earnings disregard allowed by the DSS before her benefits are affected. Fiona loved the work and got on very well with the staff, children and parents. The work went so well that the nursery wanted to offer her more hours but this would take her earnings over the disregard limit and so affect her benefits. The housing association were reluctant for Fiona to do this because it would affect her housing benefit and therefore her rent. So, Fiona's mum gives her a gift of money equivalent to the extra hours she works. This is handed to the nursery, who then give it to Fiona 'as if' it were pay, although everyone, including Fiona, knows it is from her mum.

Fiona is extremely angry about this situation. She is being offered a job which she likes and can do well. The nursery likes her and they want to employ her for more hours. But she is unable to take more hours because of the effect it would have on her benefits. She knows she needs the benefits to pay her rent but she resents having to claim something called 'incapacity' benefit, when in fact she feels very capable of doing the job. To cap it all, she has to put up with her mum giving money to the nursery, who then give it to her, all as pretend wages. It appears that no one has investigated other options with her, such as disability working allowance or the possibly of earning the higher rate of therapeutic earnings.

Mark's Story

Mark left hospital six years ago. Since then he has lived in a number of different places and has experienced being attacked, having his basic needs ignored and becoming almost a prisoner in his flat. Mark does not use speech and needs a lot of daily support but he does know what he likes and doesn't like, and he has very clear opinions about what he wants to do.

Luckily, Mark met Andrew, someone who could help him. They became friends and Andrew worked with Mark to look at the options for his life. They set up a trust fund but not of the usual sort. This trust fund belongs to Mark. It is run by three trustees who are all Mark's friends and who are committed to enabling Mark to live his life as he wants. The trust fund negotiated with a service purchaser for a direct payment so that Mark can buy his own support. (A direct payment is a payment made by a local authority to a service user in lieu of direct services. The user, and their supporters, can then use the money directly to purchase the help or activities as they want. See 'Funding Freedom', Holman & Collins 1997 for more details.) The trust also helped Mark find a house to live in and pay four people to be his employees, working with him on a 24 hour basis. They enabled him to go on holiday and buy a canal boat, which Mark has since decided to sell and buy a caravanette instead.

Mark is protected by having a trust administrator who is also his advocate. Mark and his wishes are therefore at the heart of decisions about his life and his money. There are dilemmas when the distinction between employee and friend merges but, for Mark, his particular trust fund seems to work very well.

These are all true stories, real people who experience the possibilities and the problems of money and its control. Their experiences are by no means unique. The rest of this report describes and discusses the range of financial issues for organisations, staff, families, national agencies and people with learning difficulties which these stories demand that we address with urgency.

Catherine Bewley

April 1997

Chapter 1

INTRODUCTION

Having control over our lives includes being able to make decisions about how to manage and spend our money. Most people with learning difficulties do not have much money under their control to spend. They can be poor for many reasons such as not having a job, being on benefits, not owning property or having any inherited money. However, many people with learning difficulties *do* have a lot of money paid out on their behalf to other people or organisations. People who live in long-stay hospitals and other residential settings can amass a large amount of money in bank accounts which, in theory, belongs to them but to which they have little or no access. They are often only given limited options for spending this money.

Some people with learning difficulties have other people controlling their money who do not look after it properly. For instance, some appointees have been known to misuse people's money; solicitors who act as receivers or trustees can be reluctant to approve spending on someone's behalf; and banks can refuse to open accounts for people who do not have written signatures or need additional support to manage an account. People with learning difficulties are sometimes thought to be incapable of making, or being involved in, decisions about their money. Even if someone is not able to manage their own money on their own, there are ways they can contribute to choices about how it is spent.

Values Into Action (VIA), through its *Unnecessary Poverty Project*, set out to look at these issues. Many service organisations have guidelines for staff about how to manage people's money but not how to help people with learning difficulties manage their own money. This puts staff in potentially difficult positions and also leaves the person with learning difficulties with restricted control over their money and open to possible financial abuse. In addition, there is virtually no monitoring of appointeeships by the Benefits Agency and there can also be problems with trust funds, some of which are administered by someone who might not know the person with learning difficulties very well and might have little understanding of how to involve and empower them in the process of spending their money.

VIA was also interested in what happens about money when people with learning difficulties live with their families. Contributing to the collective family income from personal benefits is perhaps an ordinary part of family life, appropriate for people with learning difficulties no less than any one else. Are families best placed to manage, or help manage, their relative's money? Or are there problems here too? More generally, VIA was interested in how to promote ways in which people with learning difficulties can have better access to, and control of, their money. What needs to change to make this happen? Clearer procedures within organisations? More education and support for people with learning difficulties themselves? Changes to the legal system of appointees, trustees and the Court of Protection?

This Report

This report presents the results of this investigation and a discussion of the dilemmas and challenges, experiences and stories shared by participants. The report is aimed primarily at service purchasers, providers, practitioners and support staff but it also has important comments to make to national bodies such as the Department of Social Security and the Court of Protection. Throughout the report there are references to key publications on these topics. The reference list has been particularly thin in the past but an increasing amount of attention is being given to money matters by researchers, teachers and practitioners. Nevertheless, many of the references cited here come out of work related to older people rather than people with learning difficulties, especially older people whose mental capacity to manage their financial affairs is disputed. This body of literature is much bigger than that specifically related to money and people with learning difficulties but there are some useful lessons to draw from it.

Also threaded throughout the report are stories from people with learning difficulties and their supporters. These experiences, as noted in the Preface, demonstrate that the occasionally dry legal and organisational issues discussed here have a very real and enormous impact on the lives of many people.

Two recent pieces of legislation may well have an impact on people's money situation. The Disability Discrimination Act, which became law in 1996, contains some protection around employment, as well as services, facilities and goods. Whether and how this will strengthen employment opportunities for people with learning difficulties is discussed in Chapter 6. The Community Care (Direct Payments) Act 1996, which came into force on 1 April 1997, provides for service users to receive directly the money that would be spent on their community care to purchase their own support. This offers one opportunity by which people with learning difficulties can gain much greater choice and control over the money associated with their support. A further discussion can be found in Chapter 5.

In addition, the Law Commissions of England/Wales and Scotland have produced reports recommending changes in the law regarding mental incapacity. At the time of writing, no formal action has been taken by the government to devise new legislation based on these recommendations but this may well happen in the future. Implementation of the Law Commissions' findings would change how judgements are made about people's capacity to manage their own financial affairs; alter the working of the Court of Protection and the Public Trust Office; and have ramifications for how the Department of Social Security responds to appointeeship.

This report can not cover everything relating to money. Based on a fairly short piece of research, there are obviously limitations to the range of issues which could be covered. Nevertheless, over 150 people from a wide range of groups, contexts and different parts of the UK were involved in the research, over a third of whom were people with learning difficulties. The variety of perspectives, views and experiences was broad but the same themes kept repeating themselves. The discussion and conclusions in this report are therefore based on a substantial and wide-ranging body of qualitative knowledge, perhaps the most comprehensive collection of views from practitioners and people with learning difficulties on the issue of personal money to be researched and published thus far.

The following chapters trace these views and experiences from national policies and procedures through to personal, day-to-day experiences. At certain points, where the discussion is long and/or complex, key points are listed in boxes. Chapter 2 sets the national scene and introduces the legal and benefit contexts which have an impact on people's access to their money. The focus then shifts in Chapter 3 to the day-to-day experience of people with learning difficulties, their relatives and support staff. Because money matters are heavily influenced by the type of housing in which someone lives, this chapter looks at organisational procedures and inter-personal dynamics in a range of living contexts. Chapter 4 discusses the organisational challenges which arise out of this day-to-day experience.

Research participants talked about a range of organisational options which could be developed to address some of the dilemmas around money. Many were interested in the potential of advocacy and independent finance schemes. There are only a few such schemes in existence at the moment; examples are described in Chapter 5. Employment issues are discussed in Chapter 6, from benefits through to the control people have over their wages. The Disability Discrimination Act has implications for future work opportunities and is discussed at the end of the chapter.

Overall, the message from this report is that changes are needed at every level and in every context relating to people's personal money. In Chapter 7, conclusions are drawn from the research and ways discussed in which change can be supported with people with learning difficulties, staff, families, organisations, national agencies, banks and through legislation. Finally, specific recommendations are listed in Chapter 8.

For those interested in knowing more details about the research, Appendix 1 describes how the work was conducted and who was involved. Literature referred to in the report is listed in Appendix 2 and useful organisations relating to money matters listed in Appendix 3. A glossary of key terms used in this report can be found in Appendix 4.

Frameworks for Understanding Poverty

Before moving onto the body of this report and the detail of the issues and stories raised by the research, it is important to briefly refer to four wider frameworks within which personal money can be understood. A key finding of this research is that many people with learning difficulties are poor and that this poverty is directly linked to them being systematically denied access to, and control of, their own money. Issues of access and control tend to be sidelined for those who can not deal with any of the practicalities around money, or even understand money at all, but, as stories in this report demonstrate, many people have proved they can make more decisions and learn more than anyone would have imagined and, even for those who can not, there are ways of bringing access and control of money very close to the individual, as Mark's story illustrates.

Framework 1: Protection

The first framework within which people with learning difficulties' money is often viewed is one of protection and the prevention of abuse. Over the last decade, the physical, sexual, emotional and financial abuse of people with learning difficulties has begun to be uncovered and frameworks for preventing and dealing with this developed. This report makes reference to the development of organisational policies which relate to this. Organisations are also increasingly aware of the need for clear policies and procedures for dealing with people's personal money. The procedures are often couched in the language of protection, both for staff and people with learning difficulties.

Protection is an important framework. People are not only at risk from theft and manipulation about their money from individuals, as Michael was (see Preface). Some people experienced the institutionalisation of financial abuse in the places where they lived. For example, there are many anecdotes about the thousands of pounds amassed by people living in long-stay hospitals to which they had no access and over which they had no control. People's individual, personal money notoriously went on items such as minibuses, equipment and even, in one case known to VIA, a conservatory built on a ward which was due to be demolished. This report is perhaps the first time that many stories of financial abuse are gathered together and published.

It is also true, though, that many of the stories told in this report do not relate to people deliberately abusing someone financially. In many cases they are trying to deal with the difficult dilemmas about making financial decisions on behalf of someone who can not make, or needs support in making, decisions about managing their money. However, although it is true that many people managing others' money act in good faith and do their best in terms of making decisions about how that money should be spent, it is also true that many people with learning difficulties are caught up in organisational systems and family practices which *they* feel restrict their financial choices. And many people with learning difficulties feel powerless to break out of this situation. They have access to very limited amounts of money, often literally a pound or two. They know they are poor and their poverty traps them within their current predicament. As Mark's story illustrates, it is possible to bring choice and control close to the individual, even for those who will never fully understand or be able to manage their money. An over-emphasis on protection, above all other frameworks, is likely to restrict people's options and, ultimately, their rights.

Framework 2: Rights

Despite the need for protection, this is not the first framework within which people's money should be addressed. Money is a commodity of power in society, as one research participant put it. Empowering people with learning difficulties to live as fully and creatively as possible, to live the lives they want to live, whatever the 'ordinary life' is that an individual aspires to, can not possibly happen if money matters are ignored.

People with learning difficulties differ in how much money is paid out in their name in benefits and services. They differ in how much they might earn, inherit or have access to via their families. They differ in terms of the local resources they have access to in their communities. However, there is often a gap - sometimes a substantial gap - between what is paid out in someone's name and how much they can actually get their hands on or influence the use of. People with appointees and receivers may only have direct access to the 'pocket money' they are given; they might have to ask for permission to buy something. Even people who are employed do not necessarily have access to their wages in their bank accounts (see Chapter 6).

A rights framework is very important, therefore, in understanding the reality of people's access to money and their experience of poverty. Policies which support the empowerment of people with learning difficulties, 'ordinary life' and the rights of people as citizens have to address money and poverty issues. Money, and its control, are at the heart of opportunities and choices. It is also important to see this framework from a disability rights perspective, making links between people with learning difficulties and other disabled people's experience of poverty (see Beresford 1996).

Framework 3: Disability and Poverty

Many disabled people, including people with learning difficulties, are poor (Beresford 1996). Disabled people are systematically denied the same access to wealth as non disabled people by the way the education, benefits, housing and employment systems operate. This is more than simply being unemployed, although exclusion from the workplace due to physical, practical and social inaccessibility and discrimination is important.

For people with learning difficulties, this situation is even more profound because people are caught up in legal and benefits systems which have the power to pronounce them incapable of managing their money, thereby giving someone else the legal power to manage it for them. Therefore, although people might claim benefits, they might not get direct access to them. Although they might inherit money or have savings, access to these might be taken away by the appointment of a receiver. They might never have had the chance to develop concepts about money which enable them to manage it, or make choices about it, to whatever extent possible, never mind opportunities for education and practical learning about money. Mistakes are often penalised harshly, under the guise of protection. An individual's access to their money, and choices about it, can be directly influenced by the attitudes, knowledge, understanding and effort of those around them, both relatives and staff. Decisions about money, even of the simplest such as the choice of a picture to put in a bedroom (a real story told in Chapter 3), can become laden with emotional, personal and financial arguments around protection and power.

It is rare to find researchers or practitioners using a poverty framework which relates the money of people with learning difficulties to that of other disabled people and other poor families and communities. A link between these frameworks is useful because it raises the profile of money in the lives of people with learning difficulties and links them into a political and social framework about poverty. This benefits both ways: people with learning difficulties are rightly recognised as, on the whole, poor people who have needs for information, education and support like other poor people; and who have similar experiences of living in long-term poor communities. Their need for information and support about debt, for example, is given a higher standing in this framework and linked to the experience of other poor people, particularly poor disabled people, rather than being simply seen as an inability to manage money because people have learning difficulties (Grant 1995). The benefits claimed in the name of the person with learning difficulties might be the biggest source of income for a poor family. Such a framework aids an appreciation of why families may try to maintain the status quo around their relative's development if they feel the family income is being threatened.

The experience of disabled people, especially people with learning difficulties, also differs from that within general frameworks around poverty. A simple comparison about the amount of money claimed or distributed in someone's name is not enough to understand the nature of poverty amongst people with learning difficulties because, as has already been noted, people do not usually have access to much or any of this money. If this fact is not recognised, misleading comparisons can be made between the opportunities available to people with learning difficulties and other poor people.

For example, a recent study by psychologists at Lewisham and Guy's NHS Mental Health Trust compared the quality of life of people with learning difficulties who had recently been resettled from hospital with people who are retired or unemployed (Hughes, McAuslane and Schur 1996). They found that the people with learning difficulties had an equal, if not better, quality of life compared to the retired and unemployed people according to a checklist filled in by the managers of the residential homes in which the people with learning difficulties lived. However, although the services people receive and their quality of life might be a great improvement on their quality of life in hospital, the study does not recognise that many people with learning difficulties have no real options about the most fundamental choices in life, such as where to live, who to have relationships with, what to spend your time on and how to spend your money. Useful political links can be made between people living in long-term poverty and poor communities, who also have many restrictions on their life options. For people with learning difficulties, there is an even greater framework of power which can have the legal weight provided by a judgement of mental incapacity, drastically and legally restricting people's rights. People may receive great services (as assessed by the service manager) but if this is not the life they want to lead, they still live in a prison, even if it is a comfortable prison.

Framework 4: Gender and Family Background

This report includes stories from men and women with learning difficulties. It is important to consider gender issues in relation to poverty. There is a substantial body of research and writing about this topic in mainstream social policy in which the factors which limit women's access to, and control of, money have been documented. Inequalities in employment opportunities, benefits, pensions, and so on have been charted across Europe and world-wide. Links with education, overt and covert discrimination, family dynamics around money and so on have been made.

However, it appears rare that a gender perspective is applied to money matters in relation to people with learning difficulties. The evidence is confused, therefore, about whether women with learning difficulties experience similar inequalities around money as other disabled and non disabled women. There are stories from this research which *may* suggest that women with learning difficulties are more likely to be over-protected around money matters than men but this is by no means clear. Further attention to gender issues would appear to be needed. Nevertheless, it seems sensible to propose that organisations, trainers and staff should be on the look out for gender inequalities in relation to money and be prepared to address them if found.

People's experience of money and what it means to them is also likely to be affected by their family background. This includes ethnicity, class and age. Again, these perspectives have, on the whole, not been considered in relation to people with learning difficulties but they might be particularly important for staff working with people who live with their families. Families may have different concepts and experiences around money in a family context than those of staff. Changing people's money situation might have different meanings and implications for them and their families. It is particularly important for staff to be aware of these possible differences when working with black people with learning difficulties and their families.

This research included black people with learning difficulties; people from different parts of the country, including rural areas; and people of various ages but there is not enough evidence overall to draw clear conclusions. Further specific work with black people with learning difficulties and their families would be useful. Certainly there did appear to be an influence of age on money: those participants with older parents tended to feel more constrained around their money and this may possibly be due to parents bringing up their offspring in an era with different approaches to the rights and potentials of people with learning difficulties, and different family values about money.

Although these issues and frameworks have been discussed separately here for convenience and emphasis, the fact is that people's lives are a whole. Frameworks around poverty and access to money need to integrate concepts and experiences of disability, age, ethnicity, gender and so on, as these things are experienced together in individual lives. Likewise, there is room for both rights and protection approaches. The importance of delineating the frameworks is to help readers be aware of the framework within which they tend to think about money and people with learning difficulties.

As noted above, this report is based on the *Unnecessary Poverty Project* at Values Into Action. The original aim of the research was to look at what stops people having as much access to, and control of, their money as possible, rather than to investigate the sources of that money, such as the benefits system. Since money is a commodity of power and opportunity, the fact that many people with learning difficulties are denied access to and control of their money is a serious hindrance to their ability to live the lives they aspire to, 'ordinary lives', however they conceive this. The project thus began with a rights perspective. Peter Beresford rightly says that a rights based approach *"highlights the way in which civil, political and social rights are undermined by poverty"* (1996 p.555). Addressing money matters with people with learning difficulties is not simply something to be tacked onto the end of a list of issues relevant to practice or research; it is fundamentally at the centre of the possibilities and opportunities individual people have to live to their full potential.

Perhaps if people with learning difficulties had full control of all the money claimed and distributed in their names, they would still be poor. As this introduction has emphasised, people with learning difficulties must therefore be included in current debates around poverty related to disability, gender, benefits and other frameworks. It must not be assumed that money is of no importance to people with learning difficulties or that they are well off because some of them might receive a range of services. Despite the fact that there are many complex practicalities and dilemmas around this whole topic, this report demonstrates that there are many practical, immediate changes which can be made to help people have more access to, and control of, their money. This alone will significantly affect people's lives.

MONEY MATTERS

Chapter

2

LAWS AND REGULATIONS - THE NATIONAL CONTEXT

> **Chapter Contents:**
> - **Current Laws about Mental Incapacity**
> - **The Court of Protection and the Public Trust Office**
> - **Difficulties with the Court of Protection**
> - **Laws in Scotland and Northern Ireland**
> - **Trust Funds**
> - **The DSS - Benefits and Appointeeship**
> - **Difficulties with Appointeeship**
> - **Banks and Building Societies**

This chapter is an overview of the national context of laws and agencies relating to the personal money of people with learning difficulties. The chapter discusses ways in which other people can obtain legal authority to manage or influence this money and, as such, sets a national framework for the following chapters. Laws and regulations around money at a national level affect people's day-to-day lives and it is therefore important that those supporting people with learning difficulties understand this national context so that potential problems can be avoided and an inappropriate use of regulations challenged.

This chapter describes current law and practice by which organisations and individuals can legally intervene in someone else's money, using examples to show the problems with present day practices. The chapter begins by looking at issues around mental (in)capacity. This is a medical and legal term but it has a significant impact on people with learning difficulties because it involves a judgement about whether someone is able to manage their financial affairs or not. Judgements about mental capacity affect the legal options available to manage someone's money on their behalf. The chapter then goes on to consider the ways in which people can legally intervene in other people's money, in particular looking at the work of the Court of Protection and trust funds. The legal situation around money in Scotland and Northern Ireland is also covered briefly. Issues around appointeeship and the Department of Social Security are considered next, followed by the national context around banking.

Many organisations and individuals who support people with learning difficulties find the whole legal and national context around money very confusing. The legal situation relating to mental incapacity has developed through case law and statute, rather than a comprehensive attempt to look at all the issues. There are only a few legal interventions which can be made about people's money and as such they are sometimes used inappropriately due to lack of other legal options. As the following chapters demonstrate, these legal options are often chosen because there are no others available, whether they are appropriate in each individual situation or not. How these national laws and the work of national agencies can be changed and improved, including relevant recommendations from the recent Law Commission report on mental incapacity, are discussed in Chapter 7.

Current Laws about Mental Incapacity

In dealing with regulations and laws about people with learning difficulties and their money, the first issue to discuss is the legal definition of 'mental incapacity' and its consequences, as the justification for interventions around money is often based on a notion of incapacity. It is important, therefore, to begin this chapter by describing current legislation about mental incapacity, its consequences, and proposals for change. This discussion is correct at the time of going to press but legislative changes might occur.

In the context of this report 'mental capacity/incapacity' is a medical and legal term. Further details about the medical and legal perspectives in mental incapacity can be found in the Law Society and BMA guide 'Assessment of Mental Capacity' (1995). It is important, however, to note the need for another discussion about the term 'mental incapacity' because a number of people with learning difficulties involved in this research who found themselves so labelled said the term was very offensive to them. It emphasises what someone can not do and, they feel, becomes a label by which others can dismiss them as less equal citizens and human beings.

Prior to the 1959 Mental Health Act, anyone living in a long-stay hospital was seen as automatically 'incapable' in legal terms (Curran and Grimshaw 1996). The 1983 Mental Health Act allows for someone to take over the management of a person's money if that person is incapable, by reason of mental disorder, of managing their own affairs. Mental disorder is defined as 'arrested or incomplete development of mind', which means, in effect, learning difficulties. What is important to note is that the existence of 'mental disorder' by itself is not enough to justify taking control of someone's money; the person must also be 'incapable' of managing their money. People with learning difficulties have often been assumed to be a *group* of people incapable of managing their money, when in fact the law does not say this. The key question is not whether someone has learning difficulties but whether they are able to manage their money, or make a particular decision.

In terms of defining incapacity, the law is not so clear. There is no single legal definition of incapacity; case law has developed around specific personal situations. In general, the law suggests that a judgement of incapacity should relate to a specific decision and people should be presumed capable of making relevant decisions, unless there is proof to the contrary. The onus is therefore on proving *in*capacity. People with learning difficulties, and their supporters, are not always given the opportunity to prove capacity. Sometimes the label 'learning difficulty' is presumed to mean mental incapacity, even if this is not appropriate.

The next question is how to prove incapacity. The Law Society and BMA guide referred to above lists a number of legal standards which can be used in the assessment of incapacity. Historically there have been three legal approaches. One is dependent on status. As indicated above, this approach uses the existence of a label attached to a condition - 'learning difficulty', for example - as proof of incapacity. This was often the approach used outside the legal context. This report contains many examples where the label 'learning difficulty' has been taken by banks, benefits officers, services and so on, to mean incapacity. This approach has been challenged in recent years by campaigning movements such as People First and Values Into Action and, indeed, a blanket approach like this is *not* supported in law.

The second approach is based on outcomes. Thus, a judgement is made about capacity or incapacity dependent on the outcomes of a person's decision-making. However, this approach assumes that there are 'right' outcomes or outcomes which are assumed to be so 'sensible' and 'logical' that everyone 'in their right mind' would make them. If someone makes another decision, with a different outcome, then they must not be 'in their right mind'. For example, Michael had a lot of money stolen from him over a number of years (see the Preface) and, although the thief was prosecuted, Michael was himself punished by having the control of his money taken away from him. There is no evidence that anyone tried to help him learn from his experience or that he was put in touch with an agency like Victim Support. Legally, the fact that he was robbed and made a mistake in trusting the thief should not have been taken as proof of his mental incapacity to manage his financial affairs.

This second approach has been heavily criticised in recent years for its dependence on value judgements. Many of us, not just some people with learning difficulties, would fall foul of this approach because of its assumptions about what is a 'normal' decision in a situation. What may seem a ridiculous choice to one person might seem logical and appropriate to another, both of them being 'capable' of making the decision but just choosing to do different things.

> *"The crucial difference between what others see as foolish expenditure and the lack of capacity to make decisions about money must be recognised. While mismanagement of personal finances may indicate incapacity, formal procedures must never be implemented just because someone makes unwise judgements or because appropriate systems are not in place to help individuals make the best use of their money."* (Jenkins 1996 p.29)

The third approach makes a judgement about mental capacity according to whether someone has understood the decision-making process in relation to the decision being made, rather than the decision itself or the label someone has. For example, if someone quite clearly understands what it means to spend all their money in the pub and have nothing for food or anything else for the rest of the week, and still chooses to do it, then legally this would not be grounds for taking the control of their money from them. Legal proof of incapacity depends on understanding the decision-making process, not the wisdom of the decision. This is the approach used in most areas of the law. Tests of capacity/incapacity should therefore vary according to the particular decision being made.

Currently, in respect of legal decisions about ability to manage money, a judgement of incapacity tends to be a once-and-for-all judgement. This approach is inappropriate for many people, especially for people with learning difficulties, many of whom have shown how much they are able to learn and develop, often against all expectations. The competencies and skills people with learning difficulties have to make decisions about their lives are not fixed: abilities develop and change as people's lives, experiences and opportunities develop and change. There will be some things that an individual can make decisions about, at a moment in time, for various reasons, and some things that they can not.

To summarise, legally, a judgement about mental incapacity can only be made by a court or one of its related bodies (such as the Court of Protection). It may use medical information from doctors to support this judgement. In practice, people in services, businesses such as banks, benefits officers, family members and so on make judgements all the time about what an individual is capable of. However, it should be remembered that this judgement does not carry any legal weight. When trying to judge what someone is capable of doing, people should remember that the law says that a judgement should be made relating to a *particular* decision and that people should be assumed to be capable until there is evidence to the contrary. The law at the moment says that a judgement about mental capacity should be based on information from the pattern of life and conduct of the person; their state of mind at that moment; their understanding of the decision-making process (*not* the 'wisdom' of their decision); and medical evidence, if appropriate. The judgement should not be based on their 'general reputation' or the existence of the label 'learning difficulty'.

This approach also applies to the capacity to make a will (called 'testamentary capacity'). Making a will is often not thought appropriate for people with learning difficulties and yet some people will be quite able to do so and may well want to decide what happens to their money and possessions after their death. The law says that someone making a will must understand, without assistance, what they are legally agreeing to in making the will. However, they can be helped by information being put in simple language and being reminded of the assets they have to bequeath (The Law Society and the BMA 1995).

Mental Incapacity: Key Points

- 'Mental disorder' (i.e. learning difficulty) by itself is not enough to legally justify taking control of someone's financial affairs. There must also be proof that someone is incapable of managing their affairs. There is no legal basis, therefore, in saying that people with learning difficulties as a group are incapable of managing their money.

- Legally, incapacity has to be proved. People must be assumed to be capable of managing their affairs until there is evidence to the contrary.

- Judgements about mental incapacity should be made about a particular decision or issue. Incapacity to manage financial affairs does not legally mean incapacity to decide about medical treatment, for example.

- A judgement about incapacity should be based on the pattern of life and conduct of the person and their understanding of the decision-making process, not the 'wisdom' of their decision. Medical evidence can be used where appropriate.

- Only courts of law, including the Court of Protection, can make a legal decision about mental incapacity. Judgements about incapacity made by other people do not have the weight of law.

- People with learning difficulties are legally entitled to make a will if they are mentally capable of understanding the legal agreement they are entering into.

The Court of Protection and the Public Trust Office

The Court of Protection is an office of the Supreme Court and also a court of law which makes decisions about the management of financial affairs of people unable by reason of mental disorder to manage their own affairs. Some of its functions are carried out by the Public Trust Office, an executive agency which also provides administrative support for the Court of Protection and deals with the registration of enduring powers of attorney and the administration of trust funds on behalf of those who lack capacity.

Applications are made to the Court of Protection on behalf of anyone who is felt not to have the mental capacity to manage their own property or financial affairs. The Court makes a decision about capacity based on an application form, a medical report and information about the person's financial affairs. It agrees to take over the management of someone's property and/or finances because they have a mental disorder which prevents them from managing their own affairs. Decisions about mental disorder and incapacity are made from evidence presented in the application forms.

Once it is agreed that the Court of Protection has jurisdiction to manage someone's affairs, it appoints a 'receiver', the person who will manage their affairs on a day-to-day basis, liaising between the individual, their carers and the Court. The Court currently acts on behalf of 33,000 people, for each of whom a receiver has been appointed. Sixty eight per cent of these receivers are relatives of the individual; 15% are solicitors; and 8% are local authorities. The Court only implements this procedure for people who have assets worth £5,000 or more.

For those with less than £5,000, the Court can issue a 'short order' or the Public Trustee (the head of the Public Trust Office) can issue a 'direction', both of which enable someone's affairs to be dealt with without the formal appointment of a receiver. The Public Trustee can also act as receiver when there is no other suitable person available.

For both applications to the Court of Protection and the Public Trustee, the 'patient' (the person on whose behalf an application is made) is informed of the application and allowed a period in which they can challenge it. The Court sends a letter of notification of the application to the proposed receiver who must hand it to the individual with learning difficulties in person and confirm to the Court that this has been done. In Josie's case (see Preface), if staff had known what to do, they could have challenged the receivership at this stage.

When a receiver is appointed, the Court will make an order setting out the receiver's duties which will vary for each individual. Part of this can include a monthly 'income' for the person with a learning difficulty, distributed via the receiver, to cover the person's day-to-day needs. Receivers are required to submit yearly accounts to the Court to show how the money has been spent. For expenditure greater than the monthly amount, receivers must apply for permission from the Court, who consider the case and agree or disagree.

There are various fees associated with the work of the Court. A commencement fee is made at the application stage; an annual fee, based on a sliding scale according to available income, is made each year; and a transaction fee is charged when the Court is involved in a major decision about someone's assets, such as the sale or purchase of a house.

An individual's assets are protected by the Court's auditing of yearly accounts submitted by the receiver and the Court's power to make decisions about capital expenditure. In addition, the Court organises 'Lord Chancellor's visits', by which specially appointed visitors make random checks on a number of individual cases each year. There are three types of visit: legal, medical and general. There are, for instance, about 1,600 general visits per year. These visits act as spot checks on the working of individual cases. Visits can also be arranged where there is a complaint about the handling of an individual's case.

The Public Trust Office also registers enduring powers of attorney. This is a legal mechanism by which someone appoints another person to deal with their finances on their behalf, either in the present or when they become mentally unable to manage matters by themselves. To make a power of attorney, the individual needs to understand what they are setting up and agree to the legal implications. For an enduring power of attorney to remain valid after someone loses their mental capacity to deal with finances, it must be registered with the Public Trust Office. This is the extent of the Public Trust Office's involvement in enduring powers of attorney. Powers of attorney are options not usually considered for people with learning difficulties as it is assumed that people do not have the capacity to make them, although some people will have the capacity.

The Court of Protection and the Public Trust Office: Key Points

- The Court of Protection is an office of the Supreme Court which has the legal authority to make decisions about the management of the financial affairs of people deemed to be mentally incapable of doing this for themselves by reason of mental disorder.

- The Court makes a decision about someone's incapacity based on application forms from the prospective receiver and a doctor.

- The person in question is informed by letter personally delivered by the prospective receiver of the application made to Court. The application can be challenged at this stage.

- The Court then appoints a 'receiver' to manage the person's financial affairs on a day-to-day basis. Most receivers are relatives of the person in question. Receivers have to submit yearly accounts and follow the duties outlined by the Court.

- When someone wants to spend some of their money, their receiver applies to the Court for access to a specific amount of money for a specific use.

- When someone has less than £5,000 in financial assets, the Court can issue a 'short order' or the Public Trust Office can issue a 'direction'. These options do not require the appointment of a receiver.

Difficulties with the Court of Protection

The Court of Protection is one of the few mechanisms by which an organisation or individual can obtain the legal right to make decisions about an individual's money. Although this can also be done through power of attorney, many people with learning difficulties are not thought to have the 'mental capacity' to make a power of attorney. This prerequisite agreement is not required to set up a receivership under the Court of Protection. All that is required is the agreement of one person and a doctor that the individual is not capable of managing their financial affairs. The law as it stands requires the Court to give weight to the assessment of mental incapacity by doctors. In many cases, the Court does not have direct contact with the person with learning difficulties.

The Court can require a receiver to recognise that someone is partially able to manage their affairs, if there is evidence for this. However, it is the receiver's overall responsibility to decide on the day-to-day management of a person's affairs and some will ignore or overlook the individual's wishes. The Court's decision is also generally a once-in-a-lifetime decision. Although in theory receivership can be stopped, to do so an individual must prove that they are now capable of managing their affairs. If the reason used to prove incapacity was the presence of a learning difficulty, then the individual will never be free of that label, however much they might develop their real abilities to manage their money.

Assessment about capacity is made by Court officers based on information provided in the general and medical application forms. It has been suggested that Court officers may have little experience or knowledge in learning difficulties and may be under a lot of pressure, given an increasing volume of work (Langan and Means 1996). As Josie's story in the Preface demonstrates, people with learning difficulties can have the control of their money taken from them unnecessarily.

The process of assessment usually takes months and can take years if the case is complicated. Alan and Tom's story, described in the Preface, indicates the difficult situation this can put some people in. Their experience also shows how much weight is given to doctor's evidence, as proof of incapacity, with no guarantee that a doctor is the best person to make this judgement. In the meantime, the individual's assets are frozen and can not be used or transferred.

Once receivership is agreed, the individual, with the help of their supporters, then has to apply in writing to the Court via their receiver for any expenditure which is more than an agreed monthly amount. If the expenditure is agreed, the money is sent to the receiver who then passes it on to the individual. The whole process takes weeks at least and can involve a number of hurdles for the individual to overcome, including persuading the receiver to put in an application to the Court, the Court officer agreeing to the expenditure, and the receiver passing the money on to the individual. In the meantime, the person with learning difficulties is not able to make spontaneous choices about spending money; everything has to be planned and waited for.

Not all receivers know the person they are receiver for very well or know much about the philosophy and practice of working with people with learning difficulties about their money.

There is no guidance about decision-making for receivers or checking of the majority of their decisions. Yearly accounts might add up but is the person with learning difficulties being supported to live life in the way they want, with as imaginative a use of their money as possible? Langan and Means (1996) suggest that many solicitors who are appointed as receivers are not the most appropriate people for this role. They can experience a conflict of interest in decisions about inheritance money when they also act for relatives. The Court of Protection, interviewed as part of this research, agreed that more training, information and support was needed for solicitors who are receivers.

The Court of Protection exists to protect the assets of people who are mentally incapable of managing their own affairs from those who might exploit them. By putting control of capital in the hands of an independent agency a person is protected against the greed of those who could profit from their money. There are some arguments in favour of this system and, as Chapter 4 suggests, it is one way in which an organisation can help an individual be protected from those with vested interests in seeing the individual's money spent in certain ways, or saved for their inheritance. However, the Court of Protection was not designed to deal with modern day situations and approaches to people with learning difficulties. Most of the Court's receiverships cover older people who have been diagnosed with dementia and it is not necessarily expert in dealing with financial issues relating to people with learning difficulties.

Importantly, this research came across examples in which the existence of receivership had *not* protected someone from financial abuse. For example, one woman who lived in a long stay hospital had a receiver who was a solicitor. The hospital bank had to write to the solicitor every time the woman wanted some money. On one occasion they did this and got no reply. They wrote again and still received no reply. Eventually, after several months, they wrote to the Court of Protection to complain, only to discover that the solicitor had applied to the Court of Protection for the money and had kept the £1,000 received. In this case the solicitor's receivership was revoked. However, as the hospital bank administrator said "*You put someone's money into the Court of Protection and you think it's safe but it's only as safe as the person who is administering it*".

As Josie's experience illustrated in the Preface, Court procedures are not always able to discriminate between valid and invalid applications. The existence of learning difficulties does not automatically mean that a person is unable, with support if necessary, to manage their financial affairs. Receivership in Josie's case did not protect her; indeed, it delivered control of her money to people whose apparent aim was to deny her access to her inheritance.

Another example came from a man whose brother was his receiver. The man was in an accident on local authority premises and was able to claim compensation for injuries. He received an amount which was sent to his receiver but the man does not know how much he received and has not been able to get access to the money. The brother refuses to pass on the information and the local authority say that, having given the money to the receiver, they can not reveal the amount because the information is confidential.

Laws in Scotland and Northern Ireland

The points discussed so far in this chapter apply to English and Welsh law. However, very similar issues arise in respect to the legal contexts in Scotland and Northern Ireland.

In Scotland, if someone is unable to manage their affairs, a 'curator bonis' can be appointed by the Sheriff Court. Two medical reports are required to appoint a curator bonis and the role is often taken by solicitors. The Accountant of the Court supervises the curator bonis. In addition, Scottish law also allows the appointment of a 'tutor dative' who acts in a similar way to a guardian on behalf of someone deemed not to have the capacity to make decisions about their life. Tutor datives are often relatives and they have the power to make decisions about matters such as where the person with learning difficulties will live and medical treatment. There is only one type of power of attorney, which continues even if someone loses mental capacity to deal with their affairs.

In Northern Ireland, the High Court and the Office of Care and Protection deal with legal capacity issues. The two types of attorney, power of attorney and enduring power of attorney, exist as they do in English and Welsh law. A similar system to receivership exists, with the High Court appointing a 'controller' who has the responsibility of managing an individual's money in the same fashion as a receiver. A recent study found that it also has the same difficulties as the English/Welsh system (Lavery and Lundy 1994 in Bradley and Manthorpe 1997 p.65).

Examples from around the UK are included as illustrations of the discussion throughout this chapter and in the rest of the report. Despite some legal differences between England, Wales, Scotland and Northern Ireland, the same issues around day-to-day experiences with money, employment, benefits, families and so on were expressed by staff and people with learning difficulties in all parts of the UK.

Trust Funds

Benefits are affected by the amount of income someone has. One way of protecting people's inheritance, savings or other lump sums of money is to set up a trust fund. Many parents are concerned about the financial provision for their relatives after their death and trust funds are increasingly promoted as a way of ensuring and protecting income for the person with learning difficulties (MENCAP undated). Trust funds have tended to be set up for this reason. They are usually of the 'discretionary family trust' form, with one or more trustees managing an individual's money and property in the individual's best interests. Decisions about these matters are wholly at the discretion of the trustee(s); the beneficiary usually has no right to receive money on demand from the trust fund (Quinn 1995).

The main difficulty with such trust funds therefore concerns the decision-making of the trustee(s). In practice family solicitors are often appointed as a trustee but they do not necessarily know much about the person with learning difficulties, their wants and wishes, their abilities and needs for support. Solicitors are not necessarily knowledgeable about learning difficulties and support services; they might never have heard about 'ordinary life' principles or other innovations in work with people with learning difficulties. They might make assumptions about mental capacity according to the general label 'learning difficulties'.

There is obviously a need for information and possibly training for solicitors and others who find themselves in the trustee role.

One problem for those wanting to set up trust funds is that no one can really predict how a person with learning difficulties might develop in their ability to be involved in their financial affairs and in making choices about their lives. People who, not so many years ago, were expected to end their days in a long-stay hospital are now living in community settings and, in some cases, living independently. Trust fund arrangements can end up restricting these opportunities. For the best of reasons, trust funds can be established to protect someone, rather than to envisage or encourage their potential for growth and change. As with the Court of Protection, people's money can become caught up in a restrictive and paternalistic system which is no longer appropriate.

For example, one research participant, Norman, used to live in a Scottish long-stay hospital. Before they died, his parents set up a trust fund for Norman so that he could inherit some money from them, with his uncle as trustee. At that time, everyone thought Norman was incapable of any involvement in his money and a trust fund seemed the best option. Whilst Norman lived in hospital, his uncle dealt with the hospital bank and in fact hardly ever saw Norman. Norman now lives in a group home and the staff have to apply in writing to the uncle for money. Rather than simply criticising the uncle, the staff realised that the uncle felt awkward being around Norman and did not know him very well. They therefore encouraged the uncle to begin to get to know Norman, supporting the uncle in this process. They understood that the uncle needed to know about the philosophy of the organisation and its approach to supporting people with learning difficulties, in order for him to appreciate why certain requests for money were made. As the relationship between Norman and his uncle grows closer, the two men not only gain a relative but Norman's access to his money becomes easier. The staff hope that, in time, the uncle will pass some of the control of the money to Norman.

In a similar example, a woman lived for many years in a hospital and her parents set up a trust fund for her with the family solicitor as trustee. Beliefs about the rights of people with learning difficulties to live an ordinary life have changed service support to people. In this example, the woman eventually left hospital and moved into a voluntary-run group home. Some time later she got married and moved into a flat with her husband. The family solicitor disagreed with her doing this but, nevertheless, with staff support she went ahead and did it. However, she still has to apply to the trustee for access to the money her parents left her. She finds this very demeaning and thinks it is unnecessary.

In both these examples, it may have been that the people involved were assumed to be incapable of ever living independently and dealing with their money but, as practices and opportunities develop, the context in which they live has changed. It may also have been the case that the parents in both examples wanted to leave their children money and a trust fund was the only way to do this without affecting benefits. Whatever the reasons, it is obviously important that trust funds are set up within as flexible a framework as possible, with the most appropriate people as trustees.

There are ways of using trust funds to bring money and services closer to the individual and more within their control, at the same time as protecting them from potential abuse and enabling them to continue to receive benefits. Mark's story , described in the Preface, gives an illustration of such a use of a trust fund. In Mark's case, the trust fund is carefully set up around a circle of friends, supporters and an advocate who are all actively involved in supporting Mark to live life in the way he wants. Mark's experience shows that it is possible to do this even with people with greater needs, people who are usually assumed to be too severely affected by physical impairments and/or learning difficulties to be involved in any meaningful way in deciding how their money is used. These sorts of trust funds can be used to receive direct payments on behalf of people (Holman and Collins 1997).

Families, friends, supporters and staff may need information and training to help them operate trust funds in this manner. Other key aspects of successful innovative trust funds are a network of people actively involved in the life of the person with learning difficulties; the role of an independent advocate; the process of decision-making between trustees, especially when there are disagreements; and the involvement of the person with learning difficulties. The auditing of trust fund accounts can be part of the agreement between trust funds and statutory authorities where payments for services are involved. Advice about setting up trust funds can be found in 'Funding Freedom' (Holman and Collins 1997); 'Sample Trust Deed' document (VIA 1995); and Walsh (undated).

Trust Funds: Key Points

- The majority of trust funds are of the 'discretionary family trust' form.

- Trust funds operate according to the trust deed. This sets out how the trust fund should run. There is no set formula about how a trust fund should operate, although there is good practice (see references above).

- There are usually between one and four trustees with responsibility for operating the trust and making decisions about someone's money. Not all trustees have knowledge and experience about learning difficulties. Not all know the person the trust fund is for very well.

The DSS - Benefits and Appointeeship

Many people with learning difficulties receive benefits from the Department of Social Security (DSS), assessed and distributed by the Benefits Agency. There are a range of benefits people may be entitled to receive (see Davis, Murray and Flynn 1993; CPAG 1996). Where people live, and especially the label given to the type of housing ('residential', 'tenancy') affect the benefits people can claim. As Chapter 3 describes in more detail, the link between benefits and housing significantly affects the amount of money people have, in turn affecting the options open to them in their daily living (Glasman 1996).

There are two ways in which someone can become involved in collecting and spending benefits on behalf of another person. The more limited method is to be an agent, by which the person receiving benefits signs their giro or benefit book giving agreement for a named person to collect their benefits for them. An agent is usually used by claimants who can not get to the post office themselves due to sickness for example. The arrangement merely gives the agent the authority to collect the claimant's benefits; it does not give them the right to keep or use the benefits. Langan and Means (1996) suggest that the agent arrangement is probably misused in practice by many agents, particularly when the claimant is an older person. It is not clear whether this finding also applies to people with learning difficulties.

The second method is for someone to be appointed by the Benefits Agency to collect and use the claimant's benefits on their behalf. The system of appointeeship works by someone applying to their local Benefits Agency office to become the appointee for a person whom they believe cannot manage their benefits on their own. The Benefits Agency considers the application and sometimes interviews the applicant, appointing them if they believe that the claimant can not deal with their own benefits and the applicant is a suitable person to be the appointee. However, the person with learning difficulties is less likely to be interviewed as part of this process. Appointees should in theory be monitored, although in practice this rarely happens and appointeeships tend to continue without check until the claimant dies or their claiming circumstances change.

There is little guidance for Benefits Agency officers or appointees themselves about how appointees should be chosen, the responsibilities of appointeeship, monitoring arrangements or dealing with complaints. Appointees can obtain a Benefits Agency leaflet called 'Caring for Someone' (1996) which outlines what appointees can do. The DSS issues guidance for benefits officers in an internal handbook called 'Agents, Appointees, Attorneys and Receivers' which is not publicly available.

Other guidance for Benefits Agency officers says that the appointee can act for someone who is entitled to benefits and is "*unable to act, for example because of senility or mental illness*" (DSS Guidance 'Persons Unable To Act', AOG Volume 2 Amendment Number 35 Ref 11058 March 1995). The appointee must be "*a body of people for example a firm of solicitors or a HA* [sic] *or a person who is at least 18 years old*" (Ref. 11059 ibid.). The officer should treat any action by the appointee as if it had been taken by the claimant (Ref. 11060 ibid.). Neither the agent nor appointee arrangement entitles other people to have legal access to an individual's savings or capital assets.

However, it is not clear that Benefits Agency officers have all the information and training they need to support their decision-making about mental incapacity. Langan and Means (1996) make this point in relation to older people but the issue applies equally to people with learning difficulties:

> "*In deciding whether to nominate an appointee the Benefits Agency has to consider whether the elderly person is someone who is 'unable to act' and their only guidance is from the Income Support manual which refers to people unable to act 'because they do not have the mental ability to understand and control their own affairs, eg. because of senility or mental illness'. The Benefits Agency is not required to seek medical evidence and appointeeship can therefore be set up without there being an independent assessment of the person's mental capacity*" (Langan and Means 1996 p.297).

The DSS considers spouses, relatives, close friends and sometimes support staff to be in the best position to be appointees. In some cases, the directors and managers of services are appointees but this is not viewed as being the most appropriate option because of a potential conflict of interest. However, this conflict of interest can exist just as much within families as it can within service organisations. Some service organisations have a policy of not taking on appointeeships and this can cause difficulties for the Benefits Agency when no one else can be found to be the appointee.

DSS - Benefits and Appointeeship: Key Points

- An agent is someone selected by the claimant to go to the post office and collect their benefits for them.

- An appointee is someone selected and appointed by the Benefits Agency to collect and use the claimant's benefits on their behalf.

- The Benefits Agency usually interviews prospective appointees but it does not interview the claimant. Appointees are not formally monitored.

- Most appointees are relatives. Although it is thought not to be good practice to select managers of residential homes and support staff as appointees, this still happens, especially when there are no other suitable candidates.

Difficulties with Appointeeship

Problems and complaints about an appointee are dealt with in the local or district office, the national office in Newcastle only becoming involved when disputes can not be settled in this way. The DSS gave the research an example of a case which had been referred to the national office. In this instance, the parent of a man with learning difficulties had stopped being his appointee when the man went to live in housing association property. However, the parent disagreed with how the housing association was helping the man to use his money and applied to the DSS to get the appointeeship back. The local adjudication officer refused and so the parent went to their solicitor and the case was referred to the DSS national office, who also refused the parent's application on the grounds that the housing association was helping the claimant use his money to undertake the activities that he wanted.

However, the research came across many other examples describing the difficulties individuals and organisations had in pursuing complaints with the DSS. There were examples from across the country in which complaints had been made to the Benefits Agency about how an appointee had been dealing with someone's money, with clear evidence of financial abuse, but the Benefits Agency decided in favour of the appointee. Because the DSS prefers appointees to be relatives, and due to the lack of monitoring of appointees, there appears to be a marked favouring of relatives and their points of view by the DSS.

For example, in Scotland an advice agency submitted a formal written complaint to the Benefits Agency about an appointee who had refused to let his brother have any use of his benefits. This had resulted in the man with learning difficulties having his electricity disconnected due to unpaid bills and going without food for a substantial period of time because his brother, who did not live with him, refused to give him any of his money. When the advice agency complained to the Benefits Agency with evidence of this abuse, officers interviewed the appointee and decided there was no problem.

In another instance, a woman with learning difficulties who lives in a group home in a rural area is forced, against her will, by her father who is the appointee to travel to the family home once a fortnight to collect her benefit money. Apart from being distressing, this journey is expensive, costing her £14 each time. The Benefits Agency refuse to stop the father being the appointee and the social services department, in whose housing the woman lives, has a policy of not taking on appointeeships.

Bradley and Manthorpe (1997) give an example of the looseness of the process of beginning and ending appointeeships. One of their workshop participants, a care manager, described a visit to the local Benefits Agency office with someone with learning difficulties who wanted to end the appointeeship connected to his benefits. The care manager described the process as "*surprisingly simple and brief*" (p.64) but Bradley and Manthorpe add:

> "*Sally [the care manager] was not asked to give any evidence or confirm the service user's abilities. At one level, she said she was pleased that it was all so easy and informal. However she did now have some misgivings that people who were extremely vulnerable might fall through this loose safety net. She also felt it might well depend on the person you happened to see at the Benefits Agency*" (Bradley and Manthorpe 1997 p.64).

There are other issues affecting people's benefit situation. There is little allowance by the Benefits Agency for those people who manage their own benefits but might have difficulty understanding Agency letters and forms. One social services department told the research about a man who was living independently, managing his benefits quite happily, but who had his benefits stopped because he did not attend a medical which they had informed him about by letter. The man had not understood the letter or the importance of the medical. This example raises issues of experience and education as well, which are discussed in Chapter 7.

Also related to benefits is the issue of work opportunities and the difficulty many people with learning difficulties have in getting access to jobs because other people do not want their benefits to change. This situation is discussed further in Chapter 6.

Banks and Building Societies

Banks and building societies are regulated but are essentially private businesses which can set their own rules about accounts. As businesses, one way in which they judge a potential customer is in terms of his or her liability. Generally, banks expect customers to have the capacity to operate an account before one can be opened in their name. Operating an account involves knowing and understanding what an account is about and being able to make transactions in various forms, such as writing cheques, using cash cards and PIN numbers, depositing money and so on.

If someone is not able to operate a bank account fully on their own there are three types of account which they can open: a joint account; a trustee account; or a third party liability account. A joint account allows two or more people to use the same account. They are all jointly responsible for the account, have equal access to it, and are liable for any use by other account signatories. Thus, an account can be in two names but only one person signs cheques. However, if one of the account holders spends the money in a way which the other account holder does not like, the second person has no come-back. Each has accepted that they are responsible for the actions of the other, whether they agree or know about them or not. If one account holder gets the account into debt, with or without the knowledge and agreement of the other, then the other account holder is just as liable for the debt.

In theory, then, a joint account enables a person with learning difficulties who can not operate an account by themselves to have an account with someone else but both people are liable for the account. Many service organisations therefore do not allow staff to open such accounts because it puts all parties in a difficult position if one party mis-uses the account.

The second type of account is a trustee account. In this case, the account belongs to the individual but is managed by the named trustee(s). These accounts require the existence of a trust fund arrangement. The third type of account is a third party liability mandate. These accounts are set up to enable a named person to operate someone's account on a day-to-day basis, whilst the account still stays in the name of the account holder. The third party is given permission by the account holder to operate the account without being liable for the debts which the account might incur.

These accounts are often used by service organisations to enable staff to practically access the account where people can not do this for themselves. The account is in the name of the person with learning difficulties but other named persons can sign on their behalf. Sometimes these accounts are written as 'XX re: YY' accounts, for example 'Catherine Bewley re: Jane Bloggs'.

In the past, people with learning difficulties did not have bank accounts: either it was not thought necessary or banks refused permission for them to open accounts. In recent years banking has undergone many changes, becoming more customer oriented. With increasing numbers of people with learning difficulties living in the community, amongst other factors, banks have had to respond to the needs of customers who can not operate their accounts entirely by themselves.

However, at a national level banks tend only to issue guidelines to local managers about whether someone can open an account. Banks will vary between branches, and banks in a local area will vary compared to each other, about whether they allow someone with a learning difficulty to open an account. With the implementation of the Disability Discrimination Act (1995), banks and building societies will not be able to discriminate against people with learning difficulties, unless it can be proved that they lack capacity to enter into a contract with the bank or building society.

The research came across examples of flexible and inflexible practice by banks. On the positive side, Dorothy's story in the Preface shows that banks are able to accommodate the specific circumstances of people with learning difficulties. The bank in this case arranged for Dorothy to use her fingerprint instead of a signature and for a private room to be available when she wanted to make a transaction. In Scotland, an organisation supporting people with learning difficulties found that local bank branches were fairly flexible about whether customers with learning difficulties had to sign for transactions, if the people concerned were from known local families.

However, the existence of a bank account does not guarantee control over money to people with learning difficulties. Some people have accounts but have no say in how their money is used. For instance, in Chapter 6, an example is given of a young man whose wages are paid directly into his bank account but his mother holds his bank books and cash card. Although considered responsible enough to work by his employer, this man does not know how much money he has and is not given the chance to learn how to use his account.

Increasing numbers of people with learning difficulties have bank and building society accounts but the implications of the way in which accounts are set up can be overlooked. For example, considerable publicity has been given to the recent transition of the Halifax, Alliance & Leicester and Woolwich building societies into banks. Part of the transition consisted of a cash payment to exiting account holders, one payment being made to the first named person on the account. Many people with learning difficulties have been denied a payment because they have a type of account described above, the 'XX re YY' account. The payment goes only to the first-named person who is usually a staff member or family member. In organisations using this type of account, usually one staff member has been the first named person on all residents' or service users' accounts. As only one payment is being made per name, many people with learning difficulties with these accounts have not received payments. One housing association gave the example of one of their house managers, who was the named signatory for the accounts of all the people in a particular home, who also had her own personal account. She thus received only one payment and was in the unenviably difficult position of having to decide who should have the money: herself or the people she worked with. There has been considerable publicity about such 'windfall payments'; the law has now changed to force banks and building societies to take disabled customers into account in these situations.

Banks and Building Societies: Key Points

- The Disability Discrimination Act 1995 says that banks and building societies must not discriminate against people with learning difficulties having accounts.

- However, people have to be able to operate an account. This means understanding the transactions they are involved in but it does not mean people have to be able to sign their name.

- People should be encouraged to have accounts in their name. Other named signatories can be used where someone can not sign their name, or another form of identification used, such as a fingerprint.

Summary - Laws and Regulations

This chapter has discussed the current national framework for people's money, including issues relating to laws, benefits and banking. None of these areas have developed primarily to address the modern context of the lives of people with learning difficulties and all therefore have to adapt themselves to the problems and possibilities which individuals, families, organisations and others experience in relation to these legal and regulatory procedures. There is much room for change and Chapter 7 discusses proposals for change to laws and national agencies.

Having painted this national picture, the next chapter takes the focus back to individual day-to-day lives and how people with learning difficulties practically experience money matters in the environments in which they live and spend their days.

40

WHAT HAPPENS DAY-TO-DAY?

Chapter Contents:
- **Organisational Procedures**
  - ◆ **Housing Associations**
  - ◆ **Social Services Departments**
  - ◆ **Hospital and Community Health Trusts**
  - ◆ **Residential Homes**
- **Independent Living**
- **Families and Money**
- **Staff Issues - Dealing with Dilemmas**

Moving on from the national context, we now consider the day-to-day experience of people with learning difficulties, their families and the staff that support them. 'Staff' in this report refers to anyone paid to support or work with people with learning difficulties. A range of organisations were involved in this research and the procedures and dilemmas from their perspectives are summarised. The views of people with learning difficulties and their families are also described.

Most people with learning difficulties, wherever they live, are concerned about money in their day-to-day lives. Organisational policies and dilemmas have an impact on individuals in relation to their money. It was the widespread experience of people with learning difficulties all over the UK that they had access to very little money. For some people, particularly those living in places with the 'residential' label, the benefits they received did not amount to much (£14.10 per week personal allowance for those in residential homes). But many others just did not know how much money was received in their name or what happened to it. Many only ever had a few pounds in their pocket, at most, and had the continual experience of borrowing money or only having a limited range of things to buy. Most received no effective support in learning about managing money but were severely penalised when they were felt by others to 'misuse' it. Many felt powerless about their money and accepted the situation resignedly because there seemed no possibility for it to change.

At a day-by-day level, the staff interviewed for this research were keenly aware of the difficulties around dealing with service users' money. They felt unsure how to support people, while policies and procedures were often unclear or not applicable to day-to-day situations. It was not so much the practical recording of money in and money out that caused difficulties but the increasing demand to be involved in the complexities of financial issues with individuals and families for which staff receive little, if any, training.

These day-to-day issues are discussed in this chapter and wider organisational practices considered in Chapter 4. Chapter 5 describes some options for addressing these organisational and professional issues.

MONEY MATTERS

Organisational Procedures

People with learning difficulties usually have quite a lot of contact with organisations. Some of these organisations house them, support them, find them work or give them activities to do during the day. In this section we are looking at the procedures organisations have to deal with money. More and more service organisations are developing staff procedures regarding individuals' money but certainly not all and, in any case, procedures do not always help staff address the more complicated dilemmas around money. This also requires training, staff support and an understanding of the organisational and philosophical approaches to people's money.

Jenkins (1996) in 'Residents' Money: A Guide to Good Practice in Care Homes' lists four basic principles which apply to people's money in residential and nursing homes. These principles provide a useful context for money matters in other housing contexts as well. The four principles are described like this:

- *Everyone has the right to have some money to spend.*
- *Having no money, or always having to ask for it, is a form of restraint and is unacceptable. It is also humiliating.*
- *An individual's right to conduct his or her financial affairs in private is fundamental.*
- *It must be assumed that people are capable of managing their financial affairs, rather than the reverse." (Jenkins 1996 p.14)*

There are four main types of organisation which provide accommodation for people with learning difficulties: housing associations; local authorities (social services departments and housing departments); health trusts (either hospital or community based); and private or voluntary housing providers. The range, type and ownership of accommodation varies between areas. Below, experiences and examples relating to specific types of housing are discussed. Following this is a consideration of money matters in families and in independent living situations, before bringing together staff issues relevant to all these situations.

Housing Associations

Housing associations now provide a large amount of residential, group home and independent housing for people with learning difficulties. They are affected by specific housing legislation and by the regulations of the Housing Corporation, the agency which oversees the running of housing associations. The Housing Corporation demands that housing associations submit yearly information about the use of accommodation, including vacant units (properties or rooms in shared houses), this information being used in part to determine the subsidy each association receives. Housing associations also have to submit yearly accounts from which the efficient running of the association is monitored.

It might seem that these wider housing regulations have little to do with the day-to-day dealings around people's personal money but they do. One housing association involved in the research said that the regulations put an emphasis on the financial efficiency of the organisation, above any emphasis on individual rights or opportunities. Housing associations will therefore tend to have clear procedures for collecting people's rent because they are assessed on this. It can be easier and safer to control people's benefit books and subtract the amount for rent directly, rather than giving the control to the individual and risking that they spend their rent money on something else.

These issues might be of particular importance for large housing associations which need clear financial systems, perhaps functioning at a national level. Although the Housing Corporation's regulations might be of no interest to individual people with learning difficulties, in practice housing associations may use these regulations to emphasise control of an individual's money, rather than freedom and flexibility for that individual. *"We're assessed more closely on our financial viability"*, says one Chief Executive, *"not on how we put into practice principles about individual rights."*

But not all housing associations feel so worried about these issues. Another housing association involved in the research talked about how it tried to give as much control to individual tenants as possible. Each tenant receives their benefits in their own name and all benefit books are kept in the tenant's home. Each week, staff go with tenants to cash their benefits at the post office and then pay the agreed rent amount into the association's account. Sometimes the house manager does this for the tenant. Every tenant has a bank account in their own name but if they can not write their own signature or operate the account by themselves the house manager is also a signatory for the account (but see Chapter 2 for how this can cause problems). Tenants have their own purse or wallet and keep some money on them which they can spend as they want without having to justify it or tell anyone about it. If the tenant wants to spend more than £10 of the money they keep in the house, then a form is countersigned by the house manager. The house manager can authorise up to £100 spending; above this amount he or she has to get authorisation from the association's finance officers.

This particular housing association does not apply to the Court of Protection for control of any tenant's money; it believes the Court offers no more protection than the association's own financial systems offer, which are monitored by the local authority registration and inspection department and the Housing Corporation, and holds up decision-making and freedom for the individual. In addition, the association does not apply to be appointee for any tenant's benefits. However, in a few cases, relatives are already appointees before the individual moves into the association's property. The association has experienced occasional difficulties getting some relative appointees to pay the tenant's rent or give the tenant their personal allowance money. The association has no legal means to get this rent money (the person with learning difficulties would have to sue their relative); it can only try to work with the families and set up agreements with them about paying the rent or, ultimately, evict the tenant.

It is easy to see some of the dilemmas housing organisations are placed in. They rely on the rent tenants pay to survive financially, and they are assessed on their efficiency in collecting this rent by their regulatory authority. The temptation to control people's money to ensure that rent is paid is great. But this clashes with the opportunity for an individual tenant to learn about rent and the responsibility to pay rent, and to have control of their income without unnecessary intervention from appointees or the Court of Protection.

These dilemmas exist on a day-to-day basis for staff working in housing association homes. The job of the house manager in particular often includes duties around collecting rent from tenants but their job is also to support the individual in their development around money.

Which part of their job should they put first? What happens when the two aims contradict each other? What should they do if a tenant persistently spends his or her rent money? The most frequently used response is to apply to the Benefits Agency for appointeeship and take the tenant's benefit books away or, more subtly, to persuade the individual to give their books to staff. Support staff are often untrained and unsupported in more task-oriented learning options with individual tenants by which individuals can be helped to learn to manage their own money, or appreciate the consequences of not paying rent.

Social Services Departments

Some people with learning difficulties live in local authority accommodation, usually group homes. In 1996, a survey by Ginny Jenkins of Action On Elder Abuse found that very few local authorities had written procedures for dealing with the personal money of older residents and service users. It seems reasonable to suppose that this is also the case for people with learning difficulties.

Social services departments are not usually the main provider of housing for people with learning difficulties but they are often involved in organising it for the person and in continuing to support the person once they have moved in. For example, in one county, the social services department (SSD) has a policy of placing people with learning difficulties in small hotels and hostels under a Sheltered Lodgings Scheme. One hundred such guest houses provide up to five hundred places for SSD clients, with numbers from one to twenty in each guest house. The scheme was devised about fifteen years ago, matching the numbers moving out of long-stay hospital with the abundance of guest houses in the region. The county SSD has devised a Code of Practice for the guest houses, which includes standards about how people's money should be dealt with. Nevertheless, the county suspects that some guest house managers keep control of residents' benefit books so that rent is easily obtained. The SSD has a policy of not becoming appointee for people it supports and thus the guest house managers often do. The SSD recognise the difficulties with this scheme but, if they become more involved in providing 'care' for people, then they fear that housing benefit will be withdrawn and the placement redefined as 'residential care'.

Some local authorities are setting up receivership or Court of Protection units as a way of getting a legal power of intervention and control over people's money, particularly in cases of conflict with families (the pros and cons of these units are discussed in the next chapter). However, there are still few procedures for social workers to follow without having to resort to these legal interventions.

On a day-to-day level, support staff working in local authority services told the research about situations in which they did not know how to intervene about someone's money when they suspected or knew about abuse. For example, as described in the Preface, Dorothy was very unhappy about the control of her money by her family. The day centre staff who worked with her had tried to persuade the family to give Dorothy more control of her money. They had also found a bank which would open an account for Dorothy and had helped her apply for her own house. However, whilst waiting for a house to become available, the staff felt at a loss about how to support Dorothy. Similarly, in Michael's story, his social worker was attempting to find out how much money Michael actually had but his family were refusing to pass on this information. It was therefore very difficult to sort out Michael's benefits in relation to the residential home place which he wanted.

Hospital and Community Health Trusts

Many people with learning difficulties used to live in long-stay hospitals and some still do. Over the last few years, more and more of these hospitals have been closed down and people with learning difficulties moved into 'the community'. In practice, this has sometimes meant moving into accommodation managed by a community health trust, the organisation which the hospital, or part of it, turned into. There are a number of types of health trust: community health trusts, which just deal with community services; hospital health trusts; and combined hospital/community health trusts. In many areas, responsibility for accommodation and services for people with learning difficulties transferred from a long-stay hospital to a specific community trust dealing with people with learning difficulties. Some people moved out of hospital into accommodation belonging to housing associations or other providers. Even when the health trust does not provide the accommodation, the health authority might contribute towards the individual's housing or care costs.

To understand patterns around personal money in some health trusts, it is helpful to consider how this was dealt with in long-stay hospitals. Most hospitals had a 'hospital bank'. This 'bank' took control of people's benefit books and received benefits in a direct credit from the DSS. In most cases, everyone's income went into one hospital account and records were kept for each person about how much of this account was theirs. Between £200 and £300 for each person was usually kept in this account, the rest being transferred to a deposit account. There could be many thousands of pounds in these accounts. Some people accrued tens of thousands of pounds over the many years they were in hospital, with usually no help given about how they might use this money for their own development. The interest on the hospital bank accounts was sometimes divided between residents, although there are cases in which the hospital just kept the interest amount. Part of each person's money, usually the mobility allowance, was often put into joint purchases of mini-buses and equipment. Indeed, other items were often jointly purchased with little real, informed permission being given by residents.

Hospital residents could usually access money from the bank by going to a specific counter during opening hours (these were sometimes as infrequent as one morning a week) or asking ward staff to do this for them. There was usually a limit to the amount they could withdraw without permission from ward staff.

When people started to move out of hospitals a number of situations occurred about their money and the hospital banks. In one example from the research where a hospital had closed ten years ago, former patients from the local area were moved into three large 'bungalow' units built on the site of the old hospital. Some were moved into smaller shared maisonettes and a residential home in other parts of the town, all owned by the community health trust. A small number moved into accommodation provided by a local housing association. At first those living in the maisonettes had their own bank accounts. In the residential home, the home manager was appointee.

Those living in the bungalow units on the ex-hospital site still use the 'hospital bank' which continued as part of the trust's finance department. The bank 'opens' one morning a week for use by residents, operating under the same system and rules as before. For a while, the arrangement of personal accounts for residents in the maisonettes continued but staff became worried about how to support people about money issues and eventually the scheme was stopped and these residents brought back under the hospital bank scheme. A more restrictive practice around money was therefore re-introduced due to staff worries about their involvement in people's money. One key factor in this example is that, for ten years following the closure of the hospital and the setting up of 'community' living options, no senior staff in the central departments or the housing services changed jobs: all transferred from their old jobs in the hospital. None were given training on how to work with residents under the new 'community' living arrangements. The director of services was appointee for all residents on and off site.

It is easy to see in this example how the patterns of the hospital bank - paternalistic, authoritarian, set up for control of money, coming out of the old long-stay hospital traditions - were directly transferred to 'community' living situations. A new services director from outside the area is now trying to change these long-established and ingrained traditions about how the organisation should deal with people's money. The new services director is bringing with him lessons learnt from another community health trust which set up clear procedures for dealing with people's money. These included detailed records of income and expenditure; formal hand-overs between key holders from shift to shift; six monthly audit checks by the central finance team; monthly checks by the unit manager; cross-referencing of receipts and bank books; and a requirement for two signatures to authorise expenditure. These procedures were laborious but staff felt that the procedures protected them from accusations of stealing, as well as protecting people from financial abuse. However, whether the residents felt that the procedures enabled their control of their money is unclear.

The continued use of hospital banks for former residents is not confined to this one example. In another area, staff based at the hospital still deal with the money of residents who have officially moved out but who are living in homes owned and managed by the community wing of the trust. In this case, the Residents Finance Officer at the hospital bank acts as auditor for the community properties, setting procedures, conducting spot checks as well as yearly audits, and offering the hospital bank as an independent finance scheme. The bank is trying to change some practices by, for example, refusing to authorise joint purchases by residents for items which the trust should provide; organising money training courses for staff; enabling daily access to accounts by residents without abolishing bank 'opening times'; and challenging abuses by appointees or receivers. When the hospital finally closes, the bank scheme will become the central banking system for the community trust and its properties.

Alan and Tom's story, described in the Preface, is an example of former hospital residents, now living in housing association property, having to travel across county to the former hospital to access their money at the hospital bank. This is inconvenient and expensive for the individuals and denies them the chance to have an ordinary bank account close to where they live. It is also extremely distressing for them to have to re-visit so frequently the site that they felt forced to stay in for years. The reason given for the refusal of the community trust to release their money is that the Court of Protection is considering their case and, until a decision has been made, the trust can not authorise any change to the management of their money. In another example, a hospital bank prevented a resident from continuing with the paid job he had been offered because it refused to allow him access to the wages which were put in his account by his employer. (See Chapter 6 for more details).

Community health trusts will often provide services for people with learning difficulties living in a variety of types of accommodation, some of it owned by other organisations. Health staff of various sorts will work with housing associations, local authorities and private providers to provide health services to tenants and residents. Some housing associations, for example, use people with a nursing background in their homes, who may be seconded from a community health trust. These staff may be funded by a health authority and their practice may have a health focus which can affect their approach to work with people with learning difficulties. At an organisational level, it can provide the health trust with an influence over how the housing organisation deals with residents' and tenants' finances.

Residential Homes

Homes with the label 'residential' can consist of anything from small group homes and adult placements to large, traditional residential homes. They can be owned and run by health trusts, social services departments, housing associations, voluntary organisations or individual owners. There are few legal regulations governing how private residential homes deal with residents' money. If appointeeship or receivership exist, then these regulations will be in force. Otherwise there are guidelines, existing principally in the form of recommended practice rather than law (see Jenkins 1996 and Centre for Policy on Ageing 1996) and there are inspections from the Registration and Inspection Unit of local authority social services departments and from health authority nursing home inspectors. However, these inspections have limited power to investigate whether someone's personal money is being used appropriately on their behalf if they have an appointee (Jenkins 1996). As the manager of one private residential home described, she is the appointee for £27,000 of residents' benefits per year, with no formal monitoring of the use of this money.

The question here is not just about overt financial abuse but also about the philosophy and approach of the home's work with individuals about their money. The home mentioned above provides a useful example. This is a small, single home, not part of a chain belonging to a bigger provider. It was set up by a local voluntary group connected to people with learning difficulties and has a management board from this charity. The home has about twenty residents living in a number of flats in a large converted residential house. The home's manager is appointee for all the residents and her daughter is the finance officer. Over the six years since the home was opened, the Benefits Agency has never monitored the appointeeships. As the manager and finance officer were more than ready to admit, there are no controls on a day-to-day basis to stop the two of them abusing residents' money. However, because they are concerned about these issues, they have themselves put procedures into place to ensure that neither one can be the second signatory for the other. Other members of staff and the management board are part of the monitoring of the work of the manager and finance officer. They have also set up an ethics sub-group to consider, amongst other things, some of the difficult issues around money.

This home is trying to bring personal financial control as close to the individual as possible, enabling residents to have bank accounts and to control their own bank and benefit books where possible. However, one consequence of this is that residents sometimes spend their rent money. When this happens persistently, even after work with the individual concerned about money and rent, the home is in a difficult position. As a small business, charging as low a fee for its services as it can manage, it can not afford to lose a lot of rent. In other circumstances, if a tenant persistently refuses to pay rent, the ultimate sanction is eviction but, in this case, the home felt they could not do that, partly because of the local scandal it might cause. The temptation for residential homes, as with housing associations as we saw earlier, is to take back the control of the resident's money.

The research came across examples of other residential situations which had different practices around money. In one place, home to about sixty women with learning difficulties, residents followed an old practice of queuing up every Saturday morning to receive £5 pocket money. Where the rest of their £14.10 personal allowance amount went was unclear. Certainly none of the residents knew that they might be entitled to at least twice the weekly amount they received.

Organisational Procedures: Key Points

- It can be difficult for housing associations to balance the financial urgency to collect rent with enabling tenants to control their own money.

- Organisational procedures about people's money are necessary and protect both staff and people with learning difficulties but they can also set up a rigid and bureaucratic system around money.

- Some people living 'in the community' continue to have their money controlled by hospital 'banks'. Sometimes, the finance systems of community health trusts have evolved directly from former hospital banks.

- The professional background of staff (e.g. nursing, social work etc.) can influence staff approaches to people's money.

- Registering a home as 'residential' changes the benefits people living there can claim. Residential home managers are sometimes appointees for residents' benefits, with little formal monitoring of their performance in this role.

Independent Living

Having looked at some of the issues relating to money matters in various organisational settings, this section goes on to consider issues for staff in supporting people in independent living situations. Staff may be from housing associations, social services departments or local authority housing departments, or community health trusts who own and manage independent housing units. Staff from community learning difficulties teams within social services departments or health trusts also support people in their own homes.

A minority of staff will be direct employees of the person with learning difficulties, via a trust fund or direct payment arrangement. Those employed directly will probably find themselves involved in discussions within the trust fund about how to use someone's money and might sometimes find themselves disagreeing with some trustees about these matters. Nevertheless, the decision-making is close to the individual and the procedures involved are those set up by the trust fund (see Holman and Collins 1997).

Independent living support staff who are employees of provider organisations will have to work within the procedures and practices of those organisations. These procedures and practices will vary in their perspectives and the amount of support and flexibility they give to staff. One specific tenancy support scheme involved in the research works from a philosophy which sees money as an essential element in a person's control of their own life and decision-making. But the scheme staff also recognise that many people with learning difficulties have little practice dealing with money in the contexts required to live independently: budgeting, paying bills and rent, making decisions and choices about what to spend or save, understanding the consequences of choices, understanding the systems and agencies connected to money, and so on (Chapter 7 has a further discussion about learning opportunities).

This is a lot for people to learn. Most of us learn it over a period of years, if not a lifetime, but people with learning difficulties, who perhaps suddenly move out of very paternalistic surroundings (a hospital or family or even a group home), have to cope quickly with all of this. People need sensitive, patient support over possibly a long period of time to get to grips with it all. As Michael's story shows, when something goes wrong about money for someone living independently, there are often few safety nets and support systems. Michael eventually lost his home and his self-confidence through the experience of being financially abused. It is difficult for staff to have a role in preventing this sort of situation, unless they have direct involvement with someone. When financial matters around independent living are thought to fail, people with learning difficulties can find themselves subject to even more restrictive practices in relation to their money (Atkinson, 1989).

In some instances, people with learning difficulties refuse help around their finances, for whatever reasons. It can be difficult for social workers and support staff in these situations to know how to intervene when it appears that someone living independently is not managing their finances. In some situations, people will reject help for one reason or another:

> "The people who sought financial autonomy seemed most at risk of financial difficulty. However, it was such a delicate and personal area that people often refused to discuss their finances at all, unless forced by dire circumstances to do so. Social workers had a difficult task. They were usually anxious to avoid financial chaos and wished to promote, instead, a budgeting system with built-in savings. Their advice, however, at best fell on deaf ears and at worst caused resentment." (Atkinson 1989 p.37).

Some of these dilemmas for staff are discussed later in this chapter, after considering families and money.

Families and Money

Not all people with learning difficulties live in accommodation provided by service organisations but many of those that do will have some involvement from family members in their money situation. Some live with family members, often parents or siblings. These people will have different experiences around money, as families differ about how they deal with money. The discussion about family contexts and money, especially relating to ethnicity, found in the Introduction is particularly relevant here.

There has been little research into the family context of money in relation to people with learning difficulties. Families are not all the same; they will have different values and experiences about money. Some will believe that what happens about money in families is private and personal. This was the conclusion drawn by a MENCAP regional worker who tried to survey MENCAP members in her local area about the money of people with learning difficulties: she had three replies to the fifty questionnaires she sent out. Perhaps also at work was a view that because people with learning difficulties do not complain, everything is satisfactory. However, many people do not complain because they do not know that things could be different, they do not know that their benefits or wages belong to them, do not know how to complain or are afraid of doing so. In some cases to complain would be to invite anger and argument, perhaps even abuse.

This is not always the case:

> *"Parents are not a homogenous group. Like people with learning disabilities themselves, they may be young and vigorous or elderly and frail; they may be comfortably rich or very poor; they may be highly articulate or unable to press their case. Perhaps most importantly, they may have very differing views and values regarding what is best for their son or daughter. There is a need for caution in ascribing a common view."* (Mental Health Foundation p.99)

The research included family members who recognised the importance of money for their relatives. One parents group connected to a hospital had helped start an independent advocacy service to assist their relatives in negotiating money matters between service providers and families. A member of this group acknowledged that families can be jealous of the amount of benefit their relative receives: they can believe their relative should not be richer than them and that their relative is incapable of making choices about money. The MENCAP worker referred to above had one reply to her survey which demonstrated a keen awareness by a parent to encourage their child (who is under 16) to develop skills and control of their money.

Families, and in particular older parents, have often been caring for their relatives for many years, sometimes with little or no support. They have taken responsibility for their relative's money over this time, often becoming appointee for the benefits. Families can be mistrustful of organisations; they know their relatives can be financially abused by staff and others and they see their role as checking up that this does not happen. They may have made decisions for their relative for many years and can find it confusing and worrying to see their relative growing in skills, independence and choice, perhaps even making mistakes about spending money. Controlling access to money is one way for both families and organisations to control the behaviour of people with learning difficulties.

> *"Some parents may need to be encouraged to foster the confidence and independence of their son or daughter. It can be difficult to break routines that have remained unchanged over many years. Some parents are unaware of the potential of their son or daughter to develop, if given the right chance."* (Mental Health Foundation 1996 p.25)

Families can feel protective of their relatives. They have sometimes seen them abused by people and organisations, and they have experienced how harsh the world can be towards people with learning difficulties. Many older parents worry about how their child will survive when they die, finance being a major concern. There is a trend for trust funds to be set up as a way of passing money and assets on to children without affecting benefits (see Chapters 2 and 6 for more information about trust funds).

Some families will not be claiming the full amount of benefits to which they are entitled (Mental Health Foundation 1996). It is often the case that individual benefits and money can be viewed as belonging to the family as a whole, with a small amount of 'pocket money' being given to the relative. Changing the living circumstances of people with learning difficulties - for example, where they live and getting a job - can change their benefits and so change family finances. The Mental Health Foundation recommend that the fact that the benefit belongs to the individual should be made as clear as possible (1996 p.83). They acknowledge how easy it is for benefits to become family income but note that this can lead to people with learning difficulties being prevented from taking up opportunities if these might affect their benefits.

These examples are not just about families taking financial advantage of their relatives. In some cases there is clear financial abuse, and indeed this research came across a number of examples of this. In these cases, the person with learning difficulties is often denied information about money coming into the family in their name. Benefits are collected and spent by relatives, as in Dorothy's story. Although many people would like help to change this situation, they also feel emotional and practical obligations to their families. One advice agency told the research about a man who had his brother as his appointee. The brother was clearly abusing the man's money but the man did not want the agency to intervene on his behalf because he liked his brother and wanted his friendship. In another example, described in Chapter 2, a sibling had been effectively stealing his brother's benefits, resulting in the man with learning difficulties going without food and having his electricity cut off because of unpaid bills. In this case, a complaint to the DSS about the brother's appointeeship was not upheld.

But in more cases it is a question of family dynamics: money in all families is not simply about pounds and pence. It is attached to behaviour, control, expectations, values, agreement and disagreement, privacy, secrecy and reciprocity. People with learning difficulties often want to contribute to the family expenses and there is no reason why they should not do so. However, what is different is that people with learning difficulties often do not have a choice about the money they contribute to the family. Their money is often seen as belonging to the family. In many cases, relatives collect benefits and hand over 'pocket money' or the individual collects their own benefits but then hands it all over to their relative.

It can be difficult for individuals to break away from families and make their own choices about money. For a start, they have often been 'protected from' the learning experiences needed to manage money at even a simple level. Staff can find themselves caught between individuals and their families around money matters. For example, the research heard about staff in one group home who had helped a resident spend £5 on a picture for her bedroom when she moved into the home from hospital. However, the woman's parents disagreed with the choice of picture and were angry with their daughter and the staff. In another example, a father was irate with the finance officer of a hospital bank for 'allowing' the resident to spend 60p on stamps.

There is therefore a real need for organisations to work with families about their attitudes and approaches to their relative's money, perhaps increasingly so as people are encouraged through community care policies to live 'in the community'. Some families will not like this intervention by staff into the family's finances, they will see the family's money as its own business and they will believe themselves the best people to make decisions about their relative's money. Without legal powers of intervention, this puts organisations and staff in a difficult position and thus it is tempting for organisations to want legal control over people's money. The dilemmas for staff in working with people with learning difficulties and their families are discussed in the next section.

As the stories in the Preface and in 'Funding Freedom' (Holman and Collins 1997) demonstrate, even people with significant support needs who might never be able to manage money can have more independence and choice about money matters than they are often allowed. Having more independence in relation to money is not about people having to manage everything themselves; many people with learning difficulties will never be able to do this. More financial independence is about more choice and control, and more possibilities to learn and develop.

Some relatives are extremely supportive in this respect, encouraging the person with learning difficulties to attend classes, have their own bank accounts and savings, collect their own benefits, and contribute to the family income through work in the same way as other family members. Many recognise the work staff do with tenants and residents in supporting individual learning and development. Some support these learning processes themselves and set up innovative trust funds and circles of friends for their relative which encourage independence.

Families can also come up against the prejudices of others when they do try to change the balance of power in relation to their relative's money situation. An eighty year old mother, caring for two sons with learning difficulties, wrote movingly to the research about the humiliation she felt in trying to open a bank account for one of her sons. She had to try five banks before one would agree to an account. "*If I had been on the street begging, I could not have felt worse*", she wrote. The importance of future financial security for siblings and offspring is a great worry for many relatives.

Families and Money: Key Points

- The benefits claimed by people with learning difficulties are often viewed as family income and people can be denied access to them. People's money is part of family dynamics.

- Many families have taken responsibility for their relative's money in their best interests over many years with little support, and they are therefore suspicious of changes to the control they have over their relative's money.

- When working to increase the control people with learning difficulties have over their money, staff will often need to work with families, developing trust and sharing success stories or challenging over-restrictive practices.

Staff Issues - Dealing with Dilemmas

It is difficult to participate in many aspects of life without access to some money. The 'ordinary life' approach to work with people with learning difficulties has to address money matters because otherwise there is no 'ordinary life' (Towell and Beardshaw 1991). This is true whatever sort of support someone needs. Money matters need to be addressed with *all* people with learning difficulties and not just those who need minimal support. In 'Funding Freedom' Holman and Collins (VIA, 1997) describe how direct payments can be used to enable people with significant support needs to live independently and spend their money in ways that they want. This is possible for people whom many said needed to be in long-stay hospital, people who will always need twenty four hour support. There is no one who should be considered 'too disabled' to be involved in their money in some way.

On a day-to-day basis, how housing and support staff work with people with learning difficulties over money matters is very important. Staff are obviously working within wider organisational frameworks, which are considered in the next chapter. This section concentrates specifically on the day-to-day decision-making and dynamics which affect money matters.

Staff are often placed in a difficult situation regarding the money of people they work with. They find themselves caught between their own views, a lack of effective organisational procedures and support, family views, and the views of the person with learning difficulties. Should they support and encourage spending or saving? When should they intervene if they think someone is using their money unwisely? How do they make decisions about what is 'sensible', 'wise' and so on. Most service staff do not have any specific training in either the legal aspects of people's money or the complex human situations involving individuals and families around money matters (Bradley and Manthorpe 1995). And yet increasingly staff have no choice but to deal with these issues on a day-to-day basis. Means (1996) suggests that there is a strong need for guidance to help staff through these difficult issues.

A risk assessment and management policy can be helpful in working through the details about supporting someone when there is the possibility of negative consequences to people's actions. Such a policy not only helps staff think through what they and the individual concerned are trying to achieve in a specific situation, but also the boundaries to acceptable risk from different perspectives. Such policies can also help identify the skills individuals with learning difficulties need to develop to reduce risk.

A properly recorded risk assessment process can also help protect staff from allegations of abuse or poor practice if the consequences of the action are negative, despite the fact that views about what is 'negative' may well differ. People learn by their mistakes, a process people with learning difficulties are often overly protected from. For them, making a mistake with money might be a painful but useful lesson but relatives and others might not agree. A good risk assessment procedure can help show that the action which led to the mistake was part of a properly planned and assessed learning experience for the individual. The risk assessment policy therefore not only protects staff from allegations of negligence but also promotes opportunities for personal development for the person with learning difficulties.

As noted earlier in this chapter, an increasing number of organisations are introducing procedures for staff to follow when dealing with the personal money of people with learning difficulties. These procedures can be useful but there is the danger that work with people around money will become bureaucratic and led by administrative demands. The dilemmas between procedures and individual flexibility have been discussed by Langan and Means (1996) in the context of older people with dementia living in residential homes. They write:

> *"What is the best combination of detailed procedures and more general guidelines? How can the finances of elderly people with dementia be protected without stifling the ability of professionals to be creative in their work with such individuals?"*
> (Langan and Means 1996 p.312)

These same questions apply equally to work with people with learning difficulties. For example, one participant in the research, Robert, had been living in a Scottish long-stay hospital since the 1930s. He moved into a voluntary association's group home in 1995. The staff soon realised how important his money was to him. In hospital Robert had very little money and so control over his benefits was extremely important to him once he moved out. Staff supported Robert to collect his benefits from the post office and, after paying any necessary bills, he kept the rest in his wallet. However, Robert's eyesight and co-ordination is not very good and he kept losing his wallet. After talking this over with staff, Robert agreed to leave some of his money in a tin in the office so that, if he loses his wallet, he does not lose all his weekly money. This is a temporary measure while a small safe box can be installed in his room. Staff also helped him buy a wallet with a chain which he could attach to his trousers. It would have been easy for staff to think that there was too great a risk of Robert losing his money for him to keep it all himself. However, these staff recognised how important money was to Robert, that it represented his freedom from hospital and his new-found control over his life. They therefore spent a lot of time with him, trying to find ways to support him without taking away his financial control.

There do need to be procedures that protect both people with learning difficulties and staff but there also needs to be a balance which enables innovative and imaginative work with individuals regarding their money. Social workers and other professionals have to deal with financial matters in a climate of increasing professional accountability around money and financial assessment, which some will feel uncomfortable with. Bradley and Manthorpe (1997) note this point, particularly in relation to the effect financial assessment for community care services has had on social work practice.

Staff also have to relate to people's families about money matters. There are a number of dilemmas around this. Family members can disagree with the approach an organisation and its staff have about money. Some can feel that staff encourage people to spend their money inappropriately, or take too many risks around money, as examples throughout this chapter have described. Sometimes staff want to encourage individuals to have more direct control over their money, such as by collecting their own benefits, but families refuse to give up their appointeeship. Application can be made to the Benefits Agency to stop or change the appointeeship but the Agency, given its favouring of family members as appointees, often refuses to do this. Likewise, organisations can approach the Court of Protection to ask for a change to the individual's receiver but it is up to the Court whether this is granted.

It is not always a staff role to work with families, or appropriate for them to do so. Staff can find themselves in the middle of family conflicts around money. For example, as described in Chapter 2, day centre staff supporting a woman with learning difficulties who lives in a group home were unsure how to stop her father being the appointee for her benefits. Although the woman has little contact with her family, her father holds her benefit books and insists that she visit him every fortnight to collect the money. The woman lives in a rural area, some distance from her family, and it costs her £14 every time she has to visit her father. The woman wants to hold her own benefit books and hates having to visit her father but he refuses to give up being her appointee. In this instance, staff have to discuss with the woman the option of making a complaint to the Benefits Agency about the appointeeship and/or working with the father to help him understand his daughter's point of view. This latter option is time-consuming and may not be within the remit of staff at the day centre.

Nevertheless, learning how to work in partnership with families is likely to be important in many situations. This will involve gaining their trust and co-operation, and sharing real success stories so that families can see that things can be done differently. Many families will want to support their relative in their development but will also want reassurance that they receive appropriate support. The Mental Health Foundation emphasises the importance for staff to work constructively with families: *"We can not stress enough the need for sensitive partnerships with parents from the start"* (1996 p.99).

A positive example of staff working with a family member has been noted in Chapter 2. Norman lives in a group home but previously he lived in a long-stay hospital. Before they died, his parents set up a trust fund for Norman so that he could inherit some money from them. At that time, everyone thought Norman was incapable of any involvement in his money and a trust fund seemed the best option. Norman's uncle is the trustee, although he has had little contact with Norman. Staff therefore encouraged the uncle to begin to get to know Norman, supporting him in this process. They understood that the uncle needed to know about the philosophy of the organisation and its approach to supporting people with learning difficulties, in order for him to appreciate why certain requests for money were made.

If family members refuse to pay rent or pay for services, organisations have few options. They can either withdraw the service or evict the tenant, which they are obviously extremely reluctant to do, or help the individual service user sue their appointee or receiver for misuse of their money. But again, this is extremely difficult because most people with learning difficulties are prevented from suing because they are seen as mentally incapable of doing so. So the only option remains negotiation with people's families, a difficult job for staff.

Bradley and Manthorpe (1997) give an example of these dilemmas. They describe the situation of a man with learning difficulties who lives with his parents. His money has always been managed by his parents but, as the man begins to learn about money and his rights through respite and day opportunities, he begins to demand more control over his money from his parents. This they give him but then the man refuses to contribute anything towards the family household budget and also refuses to pay the service charges related to his day activities. The social worker is in an awkward position. Services for which someone has been assessed can not be withdrawn. The social worker's client is the man with learning difficulties and it is part of the social work role to encourage him to grow in skills and understanding of his situation. On the other hand, the social worker can also appreciate the situation of the parents who, rightly or wrongly, have come to depend on their son's benefits as family income.

Bradley and Manthorpe discuss the reactions of social workers to this case study. Personal perspectives about rights and responsibilities, money and charging for services shape individual responses to the professional dilemmas presented. Everyone has values and views about money, influenced by family background, social views, personal experiences, behaviour, and so on. It can be difficult for staff to separate what they think personally about money from how they work with people with learning difficulties about money.

One manager from a housing association described his approach to supporting staff in thinking about the value basis of their decision-making. Rather than force procedures on people, he believed it was more effective to create a climate of awareness, questioning and discussion amongst staff in their daily work. It is important for support staff to think through their own expectations and values, before being able to think through how best to support tenants or residents. It is also essential for staff to get to know tenants and residents as thoroughly as possible, and to challenge their own assumptions about what each individual is capable of.

This sort of approach can be beneficial for managers dealing with those situations in which staff use people's money as a way of controlling their behaviour. Sometimes this happens because staff are over-worked and unsupported; controlling money becomes a fairly easy way of stopping some sorts of behaviour which are more difficult to deal with. People with learning difficulties gave examples during the research of people who have their money taken away from them because staff did not agree with what it is spent on. This often centres on the spending of a whole week's allowance in one day on items like sweets, cigarettes and magazines. Staff working in health organisations, though, might also be under pressure to address health issues. In this instance, a balance needs to be found between presenting appropriate health information to people and in allowing them the free choice to spend their money as they like.

This scenario is not necessarily simple for the staff involved. As noted above, a lot of responsibility with little practice or support can lead some people with learning difficulties to make mistakes which have negative consequences for them. There might be other difficulties, too. For instance, the person might then pester staff and other tenants/residents for the rest of the week for money. This is difficult and annoying to deal with, and especially worrying if other tenants/residents are being harassed. It requires that all staff in the home adopt the same approach to the individual to help them begin to learn about the consequences of their behaviour, and this takes time, skill, persistence and patience.

It also demands that staff understand why people might behave in this way. Many years of being denied access to, and control of, money and therefore being denied the learning associated with it, can lead people to spend in certain ways. Similarly, if people have been passive recipients of services, they learn that things will always be there. Tenancy support workers gave the research an example of one woman who had needed many months of support to help her understand the concepts of budgeting. Yet even before this, it had taken one and a half years for her to really understand that the money was *hers*, and what this meant. Coming from years in a long-stay hospital, this woman had little concept about the possession of money. It took sensitive work, therefore, by staff to get a balance between intervening to protect the security of the independent home she now lived in when she forgot to pay her rent and bills, and allowing her to learn through making mistakes.

Staff Issues - Dealing with Dilemmas: Key Points

- Procedures around money can guide and protect staff and people with learning difficulties but they can also restrict individual flexibility. Staff need procedures but they also need to be supported by their organisation to work flexibly and individually with each person.

- Risk assessment and management policies can help staff work with people about their money. Such policies need to be written so that they actively promote opportunities for learning and skills development, not solely as a protection against abuse or mistakes.

- Staff need training in both the legal aspects of money and in the complex human situations they have to deal with.

- Staff need training and support to work with, or challenge when necessary, how families deal with the money of their relatives with learning difficulties.

- Staff need management support to think through the dilemmas about working with people's money. They need the opportunity to think about their own values and concepts about money, and those of the people they work with.

- Controlling money should not be used as a way of controlling behaviour.

Summary - What Happens day-to-day?

This chapter has considered day-to-day issues for people with learning difficulties, staff and families in a variety of situations. Many of the same dilemmas and possibilities are experienced in a range of situations: procedures versus flexibility; protection versus risk; bureaucracy versus individual solutions. There are no simple solutions.

For people with learning difficulties, the financial situations they find themselves in remain, on the whole, restrictive. Of the forty five people with learning difficulties who described their experiences for this research, few had jobs or bank accounts and the control of their money. Most only ever have access to a few pounds. This severely limits the choices available to them in their daily lives. Most receive inadequate support in relation to learning about money and many are severely penalised for making 'mistakes' with their money. Many have their behaviour controlled through the control of their money. The professional dilemmas for staff and the experiences of families are complex and important but, from the perspective of people with learning difficulties, the starting point for change is pretty low.

However, there is much staff, organisations and relatives can do to change this situation. Practical, thoughtful ways of discussing these issues within services, supporting staff and families, as well as people with learning difficulties themselves, are needed. The next chapter goes on to look at some of the wider organisational responses to this day-to-day reality.

ORGANISATIONAL CHALLENGES

This chapter looks at the organisational challenges in dealing with the day-to-day issues described in the previous chapter. There is a brief introduction to the financial consequences for individuals in relation to the type of accommodation they live in. Current practice around the legal interventions of appointeeship and receivership are discussed, followed by procedures relating to registration and inspection and formal policies. The final section discusses the dilemmas organisations face at a managerial level in dealing with people's money. There is much overlap between organisational issues relating to money matters at managerial and support staff levels, so much of the discussion in this chapter relates to that in Chapter 3. However, this chapter takes a wider organisational perspective, addressing managerial matters and organisational, rather than practice related, procedures or policies about the money of people with learning difficulties.

> **Chapter Contents:**
> - **Benefits and Types of Housing**
> - **Legal Interventions - Appointeeship and Receivership**
> - **Registration, Inspection and Formal Procedures**
> - **Dilemmas for Organisations**

Benefits and Types of Housing

As noted in Chapter 3, there are four main types of organisation which provide accommodation for people with learning difficulties: housing associations; local authorities (social services departments and housing departments); health trusts (either hospital or community based); and private or voluntary housing providers. The range, type and ownership of accommodation varies between areas. The label which a particular type of accommodation carries ('residential', 'tenancy') and the type of organisation providing it affects the type and amount of benefits people living there can claim. For example, in some parts of the country there has been pressure to register all homes and placements as 'residential' homes. This brings the accommodation under the protection of the local authority's registration and inspection regulations but it also affects an individual's benefits (people living in residential homes only receive £14.10 per week personal allowance).

Second, people living in independent housing, with an additional room for a support worker, are now affected by restrictions in housing benefit regulations which reduce the amount of rent disabled people can claim from housing benefit to the same level as local 'bedsit' rates, thus threatening people's ability to stay in their own homes with the support they need to do so (for a further discussion of housing benefit see Holman 1996 and 1997).

Third, in areas where long-stay hospitals have closed, there has been a mixed development of housing between health trusts, local authorities, housing associations and independent providers. Two people might be living 'in the community' in very similar sorts of accommodation but if the home is owned by a health trust they will not be able to claim the mobility component of disability living allowance, whereas if the home is owned by a housing association, they will.

The development of housing and changes to benefit regulations therefore affects the amount of money people can claim from the DSS, the amount of money they potentially have in their pockets and thus the possibilities open to them in using this money. Although organisations are somewhat at the mercy of these governmental regulations, they nevertheless have to deal with the consequences at organisational and individual levels, for example in having to explain to people with learning difficulties why they have lost their mobility allowance or why their home might be threatened by changes in housing benefit regulations.

Benefits and Types of Housing: Key Points

- People living in registered residential homes personally receive a weekly allowance, currently £14.10.

- People living independently, with families or in group homes are eligible for the same range of benefits as anyone else of their age group who is unemployed or on a low income.

- People living independently may be affected by current changes to housing benefit regulations which prevent people claiming housing benefit for the extra space they need to house personal support workers.

- People living in accommodation belonging to, or funded by, the health authority will not be able to receive the higher rate of mobility allowance.

Legal Interventions - Appointeeship and Receivership

There are few ways in which organisations and their staff can legally intervene in, or take control of, someone's money. In many situations the legal options are not really appropriate but organisations find themselves having to take these options because there are no others.

One legal intervention is the appointee system, as described in Chapter 2, which enables an appointed person to act on the individual's behalf in the collection and use of DSS benefits. A number of guidelines suggest that house managers and residential home owners should not be appointees because this gives them too much unmonitored control over someone's money (Jenkins 1996; Centre for Policy on Ageing 1996). However, sometimes, as in the example of the small residential home in the previous chapter, there is no alternative than for the home owner or manager to become appointee.

Local authorities vary in their practice about appointeeship. Some refuse to take on any appointeeships but recognise that this then leaves a gap if an appointee is needed and can mean that residents end up with potentially inappropriate appointees. Many people with learning difficulties who come under the jurisdiction of the Court of Protection will have receivers who are relatives. Some local authorities also apply to the Court of Protection to become receiver for those in their care who have financial assets over £5,000. Receivership gives the organisation a legal route by which they can control (or protect, as many see it) someone's money. However, those organisations that prefer not to take on the role of appointee, also tend not to want to be receivers either.

Those local authorities who are the receiver for a growing number of people find the demands of this role increasing accordingly, with its related paperwork and procedures. One way of dealing with this is to develop a Court of Protection or Receivership Unit within the local authority which deals directly with all receivership matters for local authority clients. Two local authorities with such units were included in this research. Both felt that the units were better placed within social services than in the local authority finance department, where staff would have little experience of working with people with learning difficulties.

One county-wide receivership unit was set up to enable a local authority to intervene legally when it felt that there was financial abuse by family members or others towards one of its clients. The unit's director admitted that receivership is not wholly appropriate in all cases but he felt that it was one of the few ways for local authorities to legally intervene in someone's money. He saw the unit as a catalyst for better practice around people's money: it could operate with flexibility, helping raise awareness of the issues with staff. For example, one man with learning difficulties was being made to act "like a boy" by his relative who was his appointee. The relative refused to change his behaviour, even after involvement from social workers, and so receivership was seen as the only way in which the SSD could challenge the situation effectively. The unit sees money matters as part of an individual's control over their life. As the unit director said: "*In the real world you often have to step in and get powers over the purse to be able to help the person make decisions about where to live and so on.*"

Another social services Court of Protection Panel oversees all those for whom the social services department acts as receiver. The Panel consists of the head of adult services, service managers for older people and mental health, representatives from the authority's legal services and community services departments. The Panel meets bi-monthly to discuss applications from people with learning difficulties, or their support staff, for access to an amount of their money. The Panel looks at the application and decides whether to support it. If they do, they contact the Court of Protection in London for the release of the money.

An officer works specifically on Panel work and is managed by the director of adult services. Procedures for assessing and authorising payments exist, with forms to record the views and wishes of people with learning difficulties as part of every decision. The Panel currently acts as receiver for seventy people and they see the number rising with more and more people living in community accommodation as hospitals close and people live longer.

One example given by this unit to demonstrate how it can help protect people's money from inappropriate use by others is of a man who lives in a local authority group home. His relative applied to the Panel to use some of the man's money to buy a car, which they would then use to visit him. The Panel said no, that this was not a good use of the man's resources.

The Panel's officers agree that using the Court of Protection system as a way of protecting people's money is very slow and cumbersome but they feel it is the only way to legally intervene on behalf of people's money. They say it is "*a sledgehammer to crack a nut*".

Receivership units are not necessarily the answer to the problem of how to legally intervene in someone's financial situation. As existing units admit, the receivership route is not always appropriate; ironically it takes control away from the individual as a way of helping the individual have more control. The control side of the scales weighs much more heavily than the possibilities it offers, as Chapter 2 describes. Nevertheless, for organisations it is one of the very few ways in which they can legally intervene in support of an individual. A receivership unit might develop some expertise in working with people with learning difficulties and may adopt a more person-centred rather than bureaucratic approach but this does not happen in all cases. Means (1996) suggests that many organisations have ignored their responsibilities around receivership and have not supported a clear approach to its use by managers or staff. This suggests that organisations still need to develop more person-centred, empowering procedures for people with learning difficulties wanting to get access to their money and should continue to question whether receivership is necessary for each individual. This section has focused on the use of receivership by local authorities but the arguments apply equally well to other organisations.

Legal Interventions - Appointeeship and Receivership

- Appointeeship and receivership are the only ways by which organisations can take legal control of someone's money. Local authorities and other organisations vary in whether they think it is a good idea to become the appointee or receiver for people's money.

- Those taking on appointeeship will be appointed by the Department of Social Security to collect and use someone's benefits on their behalf.

- Those taking on receivership will act as intermediary between an individual with £5,000 or more and the Court of Protection in London. The individual will not have direct access to their financial assets. Requests for money will be made by the individual or their supporters to the receiver who will then contact the Court of Protection.

- Some local authorities are setting up 'receivership units' to deal with all the people for whom they act as receiver. Requests for money from individuals and their supporters will pass through the receivership unit before going to the Court of Protection.

- Receivership units are sometimes seen as a way of taking legal control over someone's money where there is the risk of financial abuse by relatives or others. However, the Court of Protection system itself takes away an individual's direct access to their money.

Registration, Inspection and Formal Procedures

Social services departments also have the duty to register and inspect certain properties in which people with learning difficulties might live. Similarly, within health authorities nursing inspectors exist to inspect nursing homes. Registration and Inspection Units, and nursing inspection units, have the obligation to check how residents' rent money is being collected and used but they do not have the authority to check how residents' personal money is handled. Nevertheless, it is increasingly recognised by inspectors that this aspect of finance is very important. One chief inspector said *"Money is the commodity of power in our society"*. He felt that independent finance and trustee schemes might be a way forward, protecting and supporting both housing providers and people with learning difficulties.

Many local authorities, health trusts and housing associations are revising their policies and procedures towards people's money, due in part to the awareness raised by studies looking at the abuse of older people and people with learning difficulties, and also to the growth in complexity around a whole range of financial issues affecting service organisations. However, recent studies by Jenkins (1996) and Means (1996) both found, in surveys of local authorities, that few clear procedures exist regarding people's personal finances. This seems doubly important given the inadequacy of existing legal options for intervention in many situations.

There are no national guidelines about what these procedures should include but most include a checklist for various occasions, particularly around recording income and expenditure. Guidelines contributed to the research varied especially in terms of the framework within which they placed financial matters. One housing association introduced its residents' finance policy like this:

> *"Finances and access to them are a key facility, valued by most people. This policy endeavours to strike a balance between providing that facility to residents, while being within an accountable framework which is in the interests of both residents and staff."* (Housing association finance policy)

In this particular housing association, all transactions are checked by the locality manager, who is also the person who acts as appointee if necessary. This takes the responsibility for appointeeship and monitoring the use of money away from the immediate staff and thus adds in a layer of protection. However, the converse is that a layer of bureaucracy is also added, potentially taking authorisation about money use further away from the individual person with learning difficulties.

A second example demonstrates a housing association providing a similar framework for staff, using different wording:

> *"The overall principle behind this policy can be summed up in the following statement:*
>> *Taking control of a tenant's money or property is a serious matter. It is important to allow tenants to manage their finances as far as they are able to and resist the temptation to take over unnecessarily. However, people who are incapable of looking after their own affairs will need help.*
> *Not all people with learning disability will be incapable of looking after their own money. The assumption should be made that they are capable until they prove otherwise."* (Draft finance policy)

Here the housing association stresses the importance of assuming that people can manage their own money until there is proof that they need some support. This approach is a positive one, which aims to keep financial control with the individual. It mirrors the legal approach to mental incapacity, described in Chapter 2: people should be presumed to be capable until there is proof to the contrary. Having a learning difficulty is not enough to prove incapacity.

In addition to an overall framework and information about appointeeship and receivership, formal procedures usually contain sections covering the following tasks: collecting and recording benefits; recording of income and expenditure for each person; a log of valuables/possessions belonging to each tenant; hand-over procedures between shifts; auditing procedures; how to apply for large spending amounts; what the organisation will contribute to individuals (such as a clothing allowance and birthday parties). Some organisations have risk assessment and management policies which help staff work through issues around the individual's use of their money (see Chapter 3).

Greenwich Social Services, in its document 'Recognising and responding to the abuse of adults with learning disabilities' (1993), places procedures around personal finance in a wider context of the potential abuse of people with learning difficulties. The definition of financial abuse includes the "*misappropriation of the individual's funds for the use of a third person, or the entry of the person into financial contracts or transactions which they do not understand*" (p.12). Financial issues are thus put in a framework of rights and consent, and related to staff roles, responsibilities and decision-making procedures. However, as Brown and Stein (1997) note, adult protection policies should express good practice, rather than be simply a list of procedures to follow if things go wrong.

Registration, Inspection and Formal Procedures: Key Points

- Registration and Inspection Units do not have the legal authority to check how residents' personal money is handled in residential homes.

- There are no national guidelines about the sorts of formal procedures organisations should have regarding people's money.

- Organisations have the opportunity to develop procedures within a framework which promotes an individual's access to, and control of, their own money. These procedures include those for risk assessment and those to prevent and deal with financial abuse.

Dilemmas for Organisations

The sections above illustrate some of the dilemmas organisations face in trying to decide how to manage people's money. There are dilemmas between the financial constraints and expectations on organisations as businesses or agencies and their desire to foster practices which encourage individual freedom and rights. If this dilemma is felt at a senior level, it is perhaps not surprising that support staff can be confused about the balance between controlling finance and encouraging individual opportunity and choice.

For organisations, a key dilemma centres around the possible use of sanctions when a tenant or resident persistently spends their rent money. A residential home manager told the research that it was difficult in one case to stop a resident from spending his rent money, partly because he appreciated that the home's final sanction, eviction, would never be enforced.

There is a dilemma here, as Bradley and Manthorpe (1997) describe, about the logical conclusion to ordinary living principles: if people with learning difficulties are to be given the same rights as citizens, do they also have the same responsibilities, and should they suffer the same penalties when they break those responsibilities? Values Into Action's view is that, provided the person really does understand the situation, then the sanction should be enforced: responsibility and respect go together. Research participants gave different views about this but they all agreed that an organisation would be unlikely to enforce the final sanction of eviction if someone persistently refused to pay their rent. It is unclear what organisations actually do in such situations; possibly the individual's money will be controlled more tightly or the organisation simply loses the rent.

Another dilemma for organisations is around the security of money. Security of money is often part of organisational procedures and staff might not have many options on a day-to-day level about what they can authorise in terms of expenditure or the safe-keeping of money. Security is also sometimes part of homes' insurance policies, another factor which can restrict options, although people's personal belongings are often excluded from such policies and so should not be affected by them. On the whole, research participants supported the idea that tenants/residents should have as much control over their own benefits, bank books and money as possible but what should staff do to ensure the security of these items?

In practice, the answer often seems to be to keep 'tins' for each resident/tenant locked in the office/staff room. People have access to this money when they want but they have to find the key-holder and ask for it. There were examples given of ways staff had tried to adapt this for those people who felt very strongly that they wanted control of their own money. In one example, a man had a little safe put in his room so that he could keep his own books and cash. The safe was bolted to the floor for security and locked. Unfortunately, the only person with a key was his 'key-worker'. Although he was physically closer to his money, he had no more access to it than if it were kept in the office.

In the previous chapter, Robert's story was described. Robert, a man in his 70s, has recently moved out of long-stay hospital after over fifty years. He told the researcher that control of his money was very important to him, a practical demonstration of his change in situation. After going to the post office each week, cashing his book and paying his rent, Robert wanted to keep all his money himself. However, he was partially blind and kept losing his wallet, with increasing worries about losing his money. After discussing things with staff, he agreed to keep part of his money in the 'tin' in the office, with the understanding that he had access to it when he wanted. Staff are now working with him to put a safe box in his room so that he can have his own key and control of the money.

What unites these examples is the demand to really understand the concepts people with learning difficulties have about money and to work imaginatively with them to find solutions to problems appropriate for whatever stage they are at in their learning about money. (See Chapter 7 for a further discussion about supporting learning). However, these examples also suggest the importance of having a clear risk assessment and management policy which staff feel competent in using. Bradley and Manthorpe (1997) found that practitioners were very aware of the need to balance opportunities for individual learning against not only the risk of making mistakes with money, but the associated loss of confidence which people can feel when things go wrong. They quote Stevenson and Parsloe's comment:

> *"Our starting point is that respect for expressed needs and wishes is at the heart of empowerment. Yet…in matters relating to risk and competence, this often has to be balanced by a responsibility to protect and sometimes to control"* (Stevenson and Parsloe in Bradley and Manthorpe 1997 p.68).

A good risk assessment policy places the opportunity to make mistakes and learn from them in a framework of 'ordinary life' but helps staff balance risk and protection for each specific occasion. Risk assessment procedures usually include sections to help staff think about the aims of the activity, the kind of risk involved, the likelihood of various outcomes, procedures for recording and managing the activity, and details of the decision-making process. Such policies support staff in this process but additional training might also be required.

Another area in which staff struggle and need management support is in contact with families who are restricting their relative's access to, or control of, their money. Staff in day centres have regular contact with people with learning difficulties who live with their families. Housing organisations have contact with the families of tenants and residents over money issues when relatives act as appointees, receivers or trustees. Staff sometimes come across situations where there is evidence that family members are abusing their power over the person with learning difficulties through control of their money.

In some cases discovered in the research, staff had complained to the Benefits Agency about the appointeeship but the Agency had sided with the family. The example was given in Chapter 2 of a Scottish advice agency which submitted a formal written complaint to the Benefits Agency about an appointee who had refused to let his brother have any use of his benefits, resulting in the man with learning difficulties having his electricity disconnected due to unpaid bills and going without food for a substantial period of time because his brother refused to give him any of his money. The Benefits Agency interviewed the appointee and decided there was no problem. The complaint was thus not acted on and the appointeeship remained.

Staff were often at a loss as to how to challenge families, or unsure of their legal rights to intervene, if the family refused to respond to discussion. As in Dorothy's story described in the Preface, staff said that they knew they could take one-sided action to support someone but they were concerned about the possible emotional abuse which the person with learning difficulties might suffer once there were no staff around to intervene. They were therefore cautious about radical interventions in case they back-fired. Many did not know whether they could legally intervene in family finances on behalf of a person with learning difficulties.

Even in less abusive or contentious situations, staff are sometimes caught in the middle of family arrangements about people's money. Often these arrangements are made by the family according to what seem to be the best interests of the individual at one particular moment, but times change and many people with learning difficulties have shown that they are much more capable of being involved in decisions about their money than families previously recognised, as Norman's story demonstrates (see Chapter 3).

A final issue for organisations is how to support the process of change to organisational and staff practices to enable people with learning difficulties to have more control over their money. Staff need a framework of policies and procedures but they also need opportunities to discuss the dilemmas and difficulties they face in their work in honest and constructive ways. They need management support for the demands and challenges of the work.

It is possible to begin the process of change in an organisation's approach to people's money. One community health trust involved in the research had invested little in staff training or development for many years. All senior management staff and community house managers had transferred from jobs in the old long-stay hospital which had shut ten years previously. No new, outside managers had been appointed and there had been no re-training for hospital staff in community styles of work. Not surprisingly, many hospital finance systems had simply been transferred to community settings A paternalistic and over-protective style of money management thus continued for many years until a new senior services manager was appointed. This manager brought with him experiences from other community health trusts about more flexible and empowering ways of working with residents about their money.

The manager recognised that he had his work cut out in changing decades-old practices. Nevertheless, he also knew that staff were unhappy with their practices but were worried about changing. He set up a five day training course which all members of staff would attend covering philosophies of work with people with learning difficulties, engaging with residents and encouraging participation, practical changes which can easily be made in day-to-day work, working with challenging needs and mental health issues, team building and action planning. The manager's style of support for staff was to help them to think about their practice in an open and questioning manner, rather than to discredit all their previous work and make them feel as if they had no skills.

This style of managing change is echoed by Towell and Beardshaw (1991) who looked at ways in which organisations could promote ordinary life approaches in their work with people with learning difficulties. Successful change to how organisations work with people with learning difficulties requires effective leadership and investment in staff. An approach which emphasises values and vision and puts people first is important.

Dilemmas for Organisations: Key Points

- Organisations often feel restrained in their options for dealing with a tenant's persistent refusal to pay rent.

- Organisations feel acutely aware of the importance of security for people's money but often this is not balanced against the individual's right to free access to, and control of, their own money.

- Clear, good risk assessment policies can help organisations work with individuals around their money.

- Organisations need to support staff in working with families around their relative's money.

- Staff may need training and support from senior managers, within a clear organisational philosophy, to work effectively with people with learning difficulties around money.

Summary - Organisational Challenges

A number of challenges thus face organisations at a wider level in their work around money and people with learning difficulties. Finding effective ways to support legally enforceable interventions in people's money situations is difficult. Appointeeship and receivership are the two existing options but, to really work, both require an approach to their implementation which uses the legal powers they offer in as flexible, imaginative and individually responsive a way a possible. Registration and inspection can also be used as a way of monitoring practices around people's money in residential homes.

Organisations also need to develop procedures for staff around dealing with money, risk assessment and management, and preventing and dealing with financial abuse. Such procedures not only need to provide practical guidelines but also a philosophical framework. Organisations need to practically support a person-centred approach so that staff can really get to know the individuals they are working with, their likes and dislikes, their needs, aspirations and dreams. Such an approach helps staff to feel more confident about supporting someone in spending their money. Staff also need supportive opportunities to question and discuss their work, to think through dilemmas and how they might be approached. Formal training might also be necessary. These are all ways in which an organisation can support its staff and those it supports in money matters.

Chapter

5

NEW ORGANISATIONAL OPTIONS

This chapter discusses a range of ways in which organisations can begin to develop or support new schemes to work with people with learning difficulties around money matters. The chapter considers four schemes or approaches which address some of the organisational dilemmas in relation to people's money: advocacy schemes; independent finance schemes; trust funds; and direct payments.

Advocacy

Independent advocacy has been suggested as one solution to the way in which people with learning difficulties get caught between the needs and views of service organisations, staff and families. Advocacy schemes already work on financial issues for some people with learning difficulties. In one research area, a hospital parents group had supported the setting up of an independent advocacy service, controlled neither by them nor the health trust, to work on behalf of people with learning difficulties moving out of hospital. Financial matters were thought to be an integral part of the advocacy scheme's remit.

Similarly, in a different area an independent advocacy scheme had been set up to support people with learning difficulties moving out of a long-stay hospital. Money problems have been a key issue that the advocacy worker has had to deal with. Alan and Robert, whose story is described in the Preface, lived in this hospital. Former hospital residents, like Alan and Robert, are having to return across county every week to withdraw their money from the hospital bank, even though most moved out two years ago. This is extremely distressing for them, in addition to being inconvenient, expensive and a denial of their ordinary rights as citizens to open local bank accounts. The advocacy worker spent time trying to find out why the men's money was not being released by the hospital bank and was told that their cases, and those of hundreds of others who had moved out of hospitals in the area, had been submitted to the Court of Protection for receivership. The delay was due to the Court's slow dealing with the cases.

In this example, the advocacy scheme had the remit to address the issue from the perspective of the ex-residents and the freedom to ask questions which other service organisations may not have had. However, for the advocacy worker to go ahead with the investigation she had to work with the co-operation of some of the ex-residents. It took quite a few months before they felt happy for her to pursue their complaint. They were afraid of reprisals if they rocked the boat, suggesting something of what they had learned about complaining when they were in hospital, and another indication of why it was so distressing for them to keep coming back to the hospital bank.

Little has been written about advocacy and financial matters in relation to people with learning difficulties. However, some lessons can be learnt from schemes working with older people. In Berkshire, the county Age Concern organisation has set up an independent financial advocacy service that works on behalf of older people. The scheme acts as advocate on behalf of someone and their money. Where necessary, the scheme can take on the role of appointee for someone. The local social services department pays £150 per year for each of the people for whom the scheme acts (Community Care 1995).

Some citizen advocacy schemes and advocate partners feel confident about taking on the roles of appointee, receiver, trustee or attorney, given the right level of contact and agreement between the advocate and their partner. However, many feel that the advocacy role should be separate from those other roles:

> "'[Appointeeship] can be of real benefit to partners living in institutional settings as the money remains with and is put to best use for the individual instead of being pooled with others or held by proprietors.' Vic, Advocacy Worker

> 'Power of attorney depends upon ongoing consent and trust…In the absence of others, power of attorney may seem better held by the advocate than anyone connected, say, with management of residential care homes and nursing homes.' Sheila, Project Worker." (Dunning, 1995, pp. 112 & 113)

Others feel these are not necessarily appropriate roles for advocates:

> "'I looked into becoming a receiver for Les, my partner. It is a highly responsible role, with costs involved. I felt that it would be better for me to work alongside a solicitor who is now the receiver. I feel that I can help to inform how the money is spent as I have a closer relationship with Les than the solicitor does. The solicitor usually agrees with me anyway - we both want the best for Les.' George, Advocate." (Dunning, 1985, p.115)

Individual advocates and advocacy schemes may well be dealing with money matters on behalf of people with learning difficulties. Individual advocates also work independently with people with learning difficulties via trust fund arrangements, as Mark's story describes in the Preface. However, what statutory and service organisations might be interested in is the use of an advocacy scheme to take on the role of appointee, receiver and financial manager for a large number of people with learning difficulties. This would relieve the organisation of the conflicts of this role and provide an independent agency to work specifically on behalf of the individual. To some extent, service brokerage schemes and independent living schemes have fulfilled this role in relation to people setting up their own personal support, and will no doubt continue to do so following the introduction of direct payments for services. Nevertheless, there appear to be few examples of the use of independent advocacy for people with learning difficulties specifically around money matters.

Independent Finance Schemes

Another option for dealing with the complex set of interests associated with people's money is to set up an independent finance scheme which can cover a wide range of financial matters. There are only a small number of such schemes, although none of them are entirely independent of service organisations. Nevertheless, interest in them is growing. Local authority receivership units and Court of Protection units (described in Chapter 4) are sometimes presented as independent finance schemes but a truly independent scheme needs to be totally separate from any provider organisation and needs to deal with wider money matters than receivership.

One example from the research is of a Residents Money Service begun in 1992 and now handling the personal finances of eight hundred residents of statutory, voluntary and private homes in the area. Staff in the old hospital bank saw the opportunity to open up an independent service, managed by the health authority but acting as an arms length agency.

Any residential home in the area can buy into a range of services offered by the scheme. There are three main options: agent, appointee and audit services. The appointee service is the most comprehensive. A home buys the service for a particular resident and the scheme then acts as appointee for the resident's benefits, receiving the benefits by direct credit transfer from the DSS into an account set up specifically for that resident. The scheme then pays the resident's rent and any other agreed bills directly from an account in the individual's name. The home holds a 'float' and an agreed amount can be spent by, or on behalf of, the resident each week without prior agreement by the scheme. This amount is usually up to £30, which is reimbursed to the home by the scheme. For spending over £30 in one week, the home must log the reasons and receipts of expenditure. For large spending, the home must apply on a specific form to the scheme. However, urgent requests can be authorised by telephone, in which case the home would incur the cost and claim it back from the scheme. There is no upper limit to this spending. Amounts spent are claimed back by the home from the resident's account held by the scheme.

In the agent option, the scheme simply acts as agent for the resident's benefits, collecting them from the Benefits Agency and handing them over to the home on behalf of the resident. In the third option the scheme does not deal directly with any resident's money but audits the home's accounts in respect to that resident's money.

The scheme employs a number of finance officers who have a specific caseload of local homes. Part of their job is to get to know the homes, the staff and the residents, so that authorisation about spending can be made on an informed basis. The scheme's manager gives training about finance to all homes which are part of the scheme.

The scheme holds the accounts of each resident signed up to the service. Up to £200 is held in each current account and residents have individual bank books and bank statements. A weekly print-out of income is sent to the home for each resident but the actual amount individuals have in their accounts is confidential and not passed on to staff or families. When individuals have more than £200 in their accounts, the extra amount is invested (according to a private tender every three years) and individual interest calculated and given back to residents. For those with savings of more than £5,000, the scheme applies to the Court of Protection for receivership on their behalf. This gives the scheme, it believes, more control over an individual's money and enables more work with them about that money, preventing staff and families having the power to impose their wishes.

As each contract is made on behalf of an individual resident, a home can choose different options for different residents, and might have some residents part of the scheme and some nothing to do with it at all. The cost of the scheme is borne by the home but the scheme believes that the benefit to the home is that all appropriate benefits are claimed from the Benefits Agency and rent is paid on time. The home does not have to deal with the paperwork around benefits, negotiate with the DSS, get into appointeeship or receivership, or be knowledgeable about what each individual should be claiming. The scheme feels that there are knock-on effects on the home which encourage higher standards. For example, the home needs proper procedures around money because it has to claim back the amounts residents spend on a weekly basis. The scheme refuses to reimburse claims that are not properly recorded. It believes that improving financial procedures in homes encourages better procedures in other areas.

The advantages for residents are that an independent scheme, working primarily on their behalf rather than the home's, is monitoring their money, protecting them from potential abuse from homes or relatives as appointees or receivers. The scheme's philosophy is that its clients are the residents and it works on their behalf. However, there can be dilemmas in relation to decision-making about what is appropriate to spend and mediation might be needed between resident and home if the two are in conflict about an item of expenditure.

Many other service organisations are interested in setting up such schemes in their area to act as external, independent agencies. Such schemes have some benefits for organisations and staff. However, there are also difficulties. Where schemes are very powerful in an area, there can be pressure for all service providers to buy into the scheme, whether this is appropriate or not. A housing association in the area covered by the above example has had pressure from Registration and Inspection officers to become part of the scheme but the association feels it can provide exactly the same service for its tenants and residents, without the cost and without the need to appoint appointees and receivers.

Another controversial area for such schemes is the requirement for those with over £5,000 of savings to go through the Court of Protection. This, as Chapter 2 described, can severely limit an individual's access to his or her money and may not be appropriate for all people with learning difficulties.

Independent Finance Schemes: Key Points

- Most schemes are not wholly independent of service organisations. They are usually only available to people living in residential and group homes.

- Schemes can offer a variety of services relating to people's money. It is usually the residential home which chooses which service to buy in for each resident.

- Schemes need to be clear who their 'client' is: is it the service/home or the person with learning difficulties? They can act as an intermediary between individuals, families and services.

- Schemes can help promote good practice around money in service organisations.

- There are usually procedures for collecting and using money. Schemes

> often act as appointee for people with learning difficulties, in which case benefits are sent to the scheme by direct credit from the DSS, rather than to the individual claimant.
>
> • Schemes tend to apply for receivership automatically for people with learning difficulties who have financial assets worth £5,000 or more. There can be problems with this approach (see Chapter 2).

Innovative Trust Funds

As described in Chapter 2, most trust funds set up for people with learning difficulties are of the 'discretionary family trust' form, with one or more trustees who act similarly to receivers, managing an individual's money and property in the individual's best interests. The trustee(s) have discretion about the use of money within the terms of the trust deed; the individual beneficiary has no right to receive money on demand from the trust fund (Quinn 1995).

The problems associated with such trust fund arrangements were documented in Chapter 2. One problem concerns the decision-making of the trustee(s), who do not necessarily know the person with learning difficulties, their wants and wishes, their abilities and needs for support. Solicitors who act as trustees are not necessarily knowledgeable about learning difficulties, support services, 'ordinary life' principles or other innovations in work with people with learning difficulties. Second, people's abilities and opportunities to control more of their money can change and develop over time but they can find themselves hampered by restrictive trust fund arrangements made many years before.

The example of Norman's story has been presented in previous chapters. Briefly, Norman used to live in a Scottish long-stay hospital, during which time a trust fund was set up by his parents with his uncle as trustee. Now Norman lives in a group home and has to apply to his uncle for money. The staff in the group home are working with both Norman and his uncle to make this arrangement work more easily. The staff hope that, in time, the uncle will pass some of the control of the money to Norman.

Other examples in the research came from women who had trust funds set up for them while they still lived in long-stay hospitals. However, since then they have moved out, got married and moved into their own flats. Yet they find themselves still having to apply to their trustees for access to their money.

Many parents will be concerned about the financial security of their children in the years to come and so trust funds are likely to continue to be used. There are ways in which they can be set up and operated which bring decision-making about money much closer to the individual and their advocates. Mark's story, described in the Preface, gives an illustration of such a use of a trust fund. In Mark's case, the trust fund is carefully set up around a circle of friends, supporters and an advocate who are all actively involved in supporting Mark to live life in the way he wants (Holman and Collins 1997). The process was initiated when Mark met someone who agreed to act as his advocate and who was able to negotiate a direct payment for Mark's assessed support needs from the local authority. This money goes into the trust fund. Mark's experience shows that it is possible to set up flexible, person-centred trust funds even with people who have substantial support needs and do not use speech.

However, they do require the greater involvement of trustees in the lives of those they make decisions with or on behalf of.

Trust funds offer a framework of legal credibility, professional accountability and stability over time, providing a firm grounding for decision-making about someone's money. Advice about setting up trust funds usually states that four trustees is a good number and that each trustee should be involved in the individual's life in some way (Walsh, undated). Trustees can be parents and relatives, neighbours and friends, professionals and advocates. A key requirement for flexible and innovative trust funds is that all the participants actively engage in a discussion about the value basis of what they are doing. Difficulties around the extent and nature of user involvement, decisions and who makes them are more easily avoided if trustees have already discussed, and are therefore clear about, the principles of what the trust fund is about.

The auditing of trust fund accounts can be part of the agreement between trust funds and statutory authorities where payments for services are involved. Advice about setting up trust funds can be found in Holman and Collins (1997), the 'Sample Trust Deed' document (VIA 1995), Quinn (1995) and Walsh (undated).

Innovative Trust Funds: Key Points

- Trust funds operate according to the trust deed. The terms of this deed are therefore extremely important in enabling the trust fund to operate in an innovative way. Trustees should discuss the principles upon which the trust fund is based and how it should operate.

- It is recommended that trust funds have four trustees who can be relatives, neighbours, friends, professionals and advocates. It is useful to base a trust fund on a circle of support around a person with learning difficulties.

- The person with learning difficulties should be centrally involved in decision-making about the use of money.

Direct Payments

The Community Care (Direct Payments) Act 1996 came into force on 1 April 1997. The Act gives local authorities the opportunity to give people with learning difficulties a payment which the individual uses to purchase or create the support they need, rather than the local authority providing a direct service. The Department of Health defines a direct payment as:

> *"a payment made by a Local Authority to an individual whom it has assessed as needing Community Care Services. The Local Authority makes the payment instead of arranging the services it has assessed the person as needing. The person then uses the payment to secure for him or herself the relevant services. So long as the Authority is satisfied that the person's assessed needs will be met through the*

arrangements he or she makes using the Direct Payment, the Local Authority is relieved of its responsibility to arrange those services for that person" (DoH 1997).

For some people with learning difficulties, direct payments will mean much greater access to, and control of, their own money, whether or not they need support to do this. Direct payments present the opportunity to by-pass existing services and all the related arguments about how people's money should be handled. People can apply for direct payments independently or with the help of a personalised trust fund, independent living scheme or service brokerage scheme. However, if an appointee or receiver exists, people may need to be supported in challenging the need for these roles with the Department of Social Security and the Court of Protection. The continued existence of appointees or receivers could undermine the potential of a direct payment to bring the control of money closer to the individual. Appointees and receivers are not necessary if an innovative trust fund is set up to help the individual make decisions about their money.

More detailed information about direct payments can be found in 'Funding Freedom' (Holman and Collins, VIA, 1997).

Direct Payments: Key Points

- The Community Care (Direct Payments) Act 1996 came into force on 1 April 1997. People with learning difficulties can now apply to directly receive the money which would have purchased the services they have been assessed as needing.

- People can be helped to get a direct payment by trust funds, independent living schemes and service brokerage schemes.

- The existence of an appointee or receiver should be questioned if someone needs a direct payment as these roles can prevent the individual from being closely involved in decision-making about their money.

- More information about direct payments can be found in 'Funding Freedom' by Holman and Collins (VIA, 1997).

Summary - New Organisational Options

There are thus a number of practical schemes which provide ways forward in working with people with learning difficulties about their money. Some of these involve setting up formal schemes, particularly in relation to creating independent third parties who can act on behalf of people with learning difficulties, providing a framework for the legal and practical aspects of money. At an individual level, advocacy, imaginative use of trust funds and direct payments all offer ways of bringing the control of money closer to the individual whilst at the same time providing a legal and protective framework. No option should be ruled out for an individual purely on the basis that they require substantial support, will never be able to manage their money independently or because they express their needs and choices in non-verbal ways.

Chapter
6

EMPLOYMENT

Most people with learning difficulties claim benefits. Very few earn their living through paid work. Even those who do work find their options restricted by the financial system they are in. This chapter looks at people's experiences around work in relation to money, from practical benefit and banking issues to dynamics around employment within families and service organisations.

Chapter Contents:
- **Why Work?**
- **Benefit Traps**
- **Family Issues**
- **Organisational Issues**
- **The Disability Discrimination Act**

Why Work?

Why are many people with learning difficulties interested in work? Wertheimer (1991) lists six positive benefits associated with employment: dignity, identity, income, wider powers of choice, opportunities to contribute, and social connections. In addition, many people with learning difficulties are well aware that working is, on the whole, seen as 'normal' in society, it is generally a valued and respected part of life and they want to share these benefits. Sinason (1995) found that people with learning difficulties liked employment, even if they did not always fully understand the financial side of it.

This research included a number of employment agencies specifically geared to supporting people with learning difficulties in finding work. Staff in the agencies emphasised the importance of their approach to this work: they all agreed that the work had to be seen as 'real' work, not a form of day care or therapy. People should be paid the same hourly rate as colleagues doing similar jobs and should receive the same protections and perks. Alongside these rights, people with learning difficulties are also subject to the same responsibilities as those doing equivalent jobs. An appropriate level of skilled support from service and employment agency staff may be needed to help people respond to these demands.

There are some difficult lessons associated with work for both individuals and organisations. In Chapter 4 the dilemmas for organisations in helping people learn about financial responsibilities were discussed; should someone who persistently refuses to pay their rent be evicted, for example? The same dilemmas exist in the world of work, where people with learning difficulties have to learn that their rights as employees also bring responsibilities, with sanctions attached to breaking rules. If someone steals persistently, an employer may be less likely to be tolerant than a housing provider which does not receive rent. People with learning difficulties have often been made passive in relation to services, and it can take time to learn that the world of work demands things which may not have been demanded of people before.

Not all people with learning difficulties find work through the help of employment agencies and agencies are not available in all areas. Nevertheless, employment agencies specifically set up, or with expertise, to support people with learning difficulties provide valuable lessons and experiences in how employment opportunities can be made available and supported. Agency staff work to create job opportunities that ensure that no one is financially worse off by taking a job. This is often a major stumbling block to people finding or keeping jobs, as Fiona's story in the Preface demonstrates. In some cases, a person with learning difficulties, given the opportunity, may choose to have less money in order to have a job.

Benefit Traps

The benefit situation is one of the most common factors hindering people with learning difficulties from getting 'real' jobs. Fiona was able to get work in the nursery attached to the college she attended. She worked the number of hours allowed before she reached the earnings limit, above which her benefits would be affected. She did so well in the job that the nursery offered her more hours but she was unable to take up this opportunity because her benefits would be reduced according to the extra income she earned and this would, in turn, affect the benefits she claimed for rent.

Under DSS regulations, people receiving income support can not earn more than £15 a week before their benefits are reduced in line with their earnings. Employment agencies insist that people with learning difficulties receive the same terms and conditions as everyone else in equivalent positions at their place of work but this means that they can only work as many hours as it takes to earn £15. This is frustrating for those who want, and are able, to work more hours and for the employers who might want to employ people for more hours.

The discounted earnings figure rises to £46.50 for what are called 'therapeutic earnings'. Most employment agencies are able to get people jobs for the number of hours it takes them to earn up to £46.50. However, having to do this under a scheme called 'therapeutic earnings' goes against their philosophy of work with people with learning difficulties. The therapeutic earnings allowance has not changed in line with wages, and therefore as wages per hour rise, people with learning difficulties are effectively forced to cut the number of hours they can work to stay within the £46.50 limit. Because they often already work as many hours as possible, it becomes difficult to take overtime when available. In addition, therapeutic earnings can lead to people losing their severe disablement allowance, if the work is seen as disproving their incapacity (Brown and Benson 1992). The research heard about many people who had to refuse promotions because of these earnings limits, even when they and their employer wanted them to do the job, as Fiona's story above illustrates.

An alternative is to help people get jobs which are paid well enough to cover all the person's living expenses, hence negating the need for benefits and thus avoiding these benefit traps. Again there are difficulties with this. The cost of living and service arrangements is often high and people would have to earn a substantial wage to cover rent and services fees. As one woman told the research: "*Unemployment is really high round here. I'd need to earn about £250 a week to pay all my expenses. If the job centre advertised a job for that amount there would be a queue round the block and they wouldn't give it to me, would they?*"

Disability working allowance (DWA) is a benefit paid to disabled people who work sixteen or more hours per week and earn less than £90, made available in recognition of the difficulties disabled people have in finding work. However, many people with learning difficulties can not find jobs of more than sixteen hours per week which pay enough to cover all the benefits they would lose. If people are in residential or highly supported housing, they are not eligible to apply for disability working allowance. The benefits system thus prevents many people from accessing the world of paid work.

> *"Supported employment services have demonstrated that with appropriate support many severely disabled people can hold down a job in open employment. Many people with learning disabilities are keen to be employed but are deterred by the benefits system and the complex restrictions on opportunities to increase their incomes. Current arrangements for financing supported accommodation for people with learning disabilities deny most of them access to the DWA"* (Davis, Murray and Flynn 1993 p.28).

Many people with learning difficulties are on benefits such as incapacity benefit, severe disablement allowance, disability living allowance and mobility allowance which require medical proof of incapacity for qualification. If people are 'incapable' and thus receiving these benefits, how can they be 'capable' of working? Except in the case of disability working allowance, which has a two year period in which people can revert to their benefits if the job ends or breaks down for some reason, there can be real difficulties in trying to prove incapacity if someone has to reclaim these benefits.

Those living in residential housing get higher benefits to pay for these services, although the amount in the individual's pocket is less (the personal allowance rate). By getting a job, the individual might have more money in their pocket but it is very difficult to earn enough to pay the high amounts of residential fees. Residential care implies that someone needs such a level of support that they should not, in theory, be capable of working. However, people can end up living in residential homes for a number of reasons, not necessarily because they need a lot of 'care'. Sometimes this is simply where they were placed when they moved out of long-stay hospital or it was the only option available. In other instances, it was thought by families or services that people needed a lot of support but, over time, they have been able to grow and develop in ways which others could not envisage. Some housing providers will call a property a residential home to be able to set higher fee rates and some authorities have placed people in residential homes as a way of reducing service costs because the fees used to be paid by the Department of Social Security.

Davis, Murray and Flynn (1993) describe the experience of one of their research participants, Robin, who lives in a residential placement and receives severe disablement allowance and income support. Robin has a severe learning difficulty and requires considerable support but he was able to get a work experience placement with a local garage. This experience really helped him make progress in expressing himself and developing his self-confidence and, consequently, his aggressive behaviour reduced considerably. After a while, the garage owner wanted to offer Robin a full-time job at the garage but Robin was unable to accept this because he would lose his benefits and therefore his housing because he would not earn enough to pay for a fairly highly supported residential placement.

Holding down a job also requires some experience, skills, confidence and sometimes qualifications. Many people with learning difficulties have been denied real job experience and so need to progress slowly. The decision to come off benefits and find work is therefore a tricky one. Families and housing providers are often concerned about the risk to benefits income if a job does not work out; at least benefits are regular, can generally be relied upon and can be controlled by others through appointeeship, whereas jobs are much less secure. Examples were given to the research of people with learning difficulties who had been offered jobs but their families or housing provider had threatened not to support them if they took the job (see below for a further discussion about family issues).

Some people receive housing benefit, which will be affected if they take a job. Re-applying for housing benefit is a notoriously slow process. In the meantime, individuals, families and housing providers are paying for the costs of someone's rent or they are getting into arrears.

In the face of these dilemmas, many organisations and families prefer not to take the risk around jobs and thus most people find themselves having to work within the financial limits of therapeutic earnings or the income disregard, even if this limits their opportunities. It is easy, though, to see how frustrating and undermining it is for people like Robin who want work but find they can not take up jobs when they are offered. Employment agencies suggest that a change is needed to the benefits system introducing a sliding scale of income and benefits, from total benefits at one end to total earnings at the other. This would enable people to progress up and down at their own pace. Following its study of the financial circumstances of people with learning difficulties (Davis, Murray and Flynn 1993), the National Development Team also recommended that the Benefits Agency pilot a benefits waiver scheme to enable people to retain some benefits income whilst receiving wages. Such changes to the benefits system are also recommended by the Mental Health Foundation (1996 p.81).

Benefit Traps: Key Issues

- There are two main ways by which people can earn some money without affecting their benefits: the £15 income disregard (for those on income support) and the £46.50 therapeutic earnings (medical evidence required).

- Disability working allowance is paid to disabled people who work 16+ hours per week and earn under £90. DWA has a grace period of two years in which people can return to their previous benefits if they can not continue with the job for some reason.

- People are often prevented from taking on more work because of the consequent reduction in their benefits, especially benefits covering rent and fees. Families and organisations can overtly or covertly persuade people not to take up job offers because of this.

Family Issues

Chapter 3 discussed a number of issues about money for people living with relatives. An individual's benefits are often viewed as family income. Benefits are a fairly consistent and protected source of income and so become a regular and stable part of the family income. Employment agencies noted that the benefits received by the person with a learning difficulty can sometimes be the biggest source of family income. There are therefore risks for families in supporting their relatives to get a job, particularly if this means that they lose some of their benefits. One employment agency involved in the research had even received threats from a parent that, if they helped their relative get a job, they would throw the relative out of the home.

On the other hand, there are many families which support and encourage their relatives to get work because they recognise the importance of both the experience of work and the opportunity to contribute to the family's finances. For example, Stephen is a teenager who lives with his parents on a large council estate in Scotland. With the help of the local employment agency Stephen found a job in MacDonalds for four hours a day, five days a week. He earns £100 a week which is paid directly into his bank account. Like Stephen, Andrea also works, earning £130 a week which is paid directly into her bank account. Stephen and Andrea are both keen to work and generally get on well with their jobs. Working gives their lives a structure; they participate financially in the family, learn independence, new skills and grow in confidence.

However, neither of them actually control their wages. In both examples, Stephen and Andrea's mothers hold their bank account cash cards and give them 'pocket money' each week. Neither Stephen nor Andrea knew exactly how much money they have or what it is used for. An opportunity, then, to learn about paying rent or board and lodging to their family, and contributing to household bills, is missed by this control being taken away.

Employment agencies work from the perspective that, with the right training, support and experience, people can learn and grow in their abilities at work. Agencies told the research that they felt it was a shame that, even when people are trusted by employers to be responsible enough to do a job, families and service organisations do not think they are able to learn how to manage, or at least be centrally involved in, their own money.

Organisational Issues

The previous discussion relating to families can be applied equally well to service organisations and staff. Employment agencies also come across restrictions from service organisations in relation to finding jobs for people with learning difficulties. Some of these relate to financial matters, as discussed above.

However, as in families, there are also attitudes and practices in organisations which prevent people taking up job options. Some of these attitudes relate to who is capable of working. Even those who clearly express the desire to try a job are sometimes prevented from doing so by staff telling them they are not capable. Practically, housing support staff may have to design an approach to working which responds flexibly to the different timetables of each tenant or resident if they work. It also demands that staff are aware of a tenant's or resident's work situation and are prepared to tackle problems on their behalf if they arise. For example, one woman told the research that she had worked for twenty six weeks without getting paid but she had not known how to tackle this herself. No one in the home where she lived had thought to check with her about her wages. It was not until the researcher asked about work at the advocacy group meeting which she attended that this situation came to light.

MONEY MATTERS

The red tape around work, wages and benefits may make staff reluctant to support someone in getting or keeping a job, or present seemingly insurmountable barriers. In another example, a man living in a Scottish long-stay hospital was helped to get a part-time job by the resettlement team. His social worker hoped his wages could be paid directly to him, by-passing the hospital bank which has fairly rigid and paternalistic procedures for accessing the money. However, the social work department, his employer, only pays wages by direct credit transfer into a bank account and the residents' affairs manager at the hospital refused to permit ward staff to help the man open a bank account outside the hospital. The ward staff went ahead and opened the account anyway but they are not permitted to accompany the man to the bank and he is unable to go there by himself. His social worker therefore has to go with him to get the money, although this is not her official role either. The man is stuck between two bureaucracies, able and willing to work and have an ordinary bank account in preparation for life outside the hospital, but presented with obstacles to his independence.

Wages may also become just another form of income which is controlled, deliberately or simply without thought. One man with learning difficulties said that the residential home manager kept the wages of those who worked in the office safe without their consent and they were unable to get access to their money. Sometimes it took a few days before they were able to cash their wage cheques at their banks. In another example from Wales, a man living in an independent residential home after moving out of long-stay hospital was able to get a job with the support of an employment agency. He was very excited about this new experience and looked forward to the options his wages would give him. For many years he had wanted a barometer and so he decided to save his wages for a while in order to buy one, which he was eventually able to do. However, the staff in his home laughed at the idea of a barometer, told him it was a waste of money and made him send it back to the shop. These examples demonstrate that getting a job does not necessarily change the restrictive practices around finances which many people with learning difficulties have to cope with from others. The staff and organisational issues which were discussed in Chapters 3 and 4 apply whether someone gets their income from benefits or wages.

In addition, learning about work is sometimes a slow process, which will undoubtedly at times mean making mistakes, feeling unconfident, practical problems (like transport and time-keeping), and experiencing conflict, prejudice and personal clashes at work. All of this will demand staff time and support for the tenant/resident to work through the situation, learn from it and make decisions about themselves out of it. As people's experiences widen, they learn about themselves and this process of self-growth is not always easy or smooth. Staff may not have the experience, skills, support or appropriate attitudes to deal with this. It might well bring a new set of issues for staff - new learning and self-growth that *they* have do in *their* jobs - and this requires management recognition and support.

As discussed in Chapter 3, there are increasing demands on staff to work within the complexities of benefits, service charges, different housing options and the dynamics of family finances. This requires knowledge, skills and sensitivity, and practitioners do not always feel supported by their organisations in coping with all of this. As well as supporting people with learning difficulties through the complexity of benefits and wages, staff also have to give emotional and practical support when things do not work out.

Davis, Murray and Flynn (1993) provide another useful example of this from their study. They tell the story of Esmin, a young woman who has a mild learning difficulty who lived with her mother and received severe disablement allowance (SDA). However, Esmin's mother died and she was assessed as needing a residential placement. She claimed income support, along with the SDA, to pay the fees. Esmin went on an employment training scheme in a restaurant and was eventually offered a permanent job there. She earned £85 per week after tax but this meant that she could not afford the residential fees at £155 a week, so she decided to move into independent accommodation and claim housing benefit.

However, the fairly sudden changes in her life have put some pressures on Esmin. Her job and the travelling, living alone and having little company and little money to go out, are all taking their toll. Esmin is becoming quite depressed and her employer is concerned about the deterioration in her appearance and her lack of energy. Esmin wants to keep her job but her social worker is concerned that she might not cope living independently. However, the fact that she does work and live alone probably means that she would not now be assessed as needing a residential place and therefore she could not move back into the residential home. She is not eligible for disability working allowance because it is more than eight weeks since she claimed the qualifying benefit of severe disablement allowance, a fact which should have been acted on by her social worker. It appears that one option for Esmin would be to create more social networks but her weekly disposable income calculated at 97p drastically limits her ability to go out and about.

Esmin's social worker therefore has to work imaginatively to help Esmin find ways around the financial situation she finds herself in. Given the skills and effort needed to support Esmin in her current situation, it is possible to see how staff might be tempted to persuade people not to take jobs and live independently. The rigidity of the benefits system and the pressures of life on a low wage make it very difficult for many people to take jobs, and threatens their ability to manage even if, like Esmin, they are keen and able to work.

At a wider organisational level, changes to local authority service contracts in some areas are starting to affect the work of employment agencies. For example, in one area the employment agency could only survive by agreeing a funding contract with the local authority by which all referrals to their service had to be made via care managers. This denied those without social workers from receiving the help of the employment agency.

Organisational Issues: Key Points

- If people with learning difficulties are to be supported in getting and keeping jobs, staff need to work flexibly with their emotional and practical needs around work and the learning experience work offers. Staff need to be prepared to deal with problems on people's behalf when necessary.

- Issues about people's access to, and control of, their money as discussed in Chapter 3 apply equally to their access to, and control of, their wages.

- Staff themselves need training and support to cope with the red tape around work matters, particularly in relation to benefits.

The Disability Discrimination Act

The Disability Discrimination Act came into force on the 2 December 1996 and brought with it an increased protection against the discrimination experienced by disabled people in the workplace and in the provision of goods, services and facilities. It lays out six broad areas in which people must not be discriminated against purely on the grounds of their impairment or other people's reaction to it. Disabled people, including people with learning difficulties, will have a right:

- not to be discriminated against in relation to employment (except where exemption applies);

- not to be discriminated against in relation to the benefits of membership of a trade organisation;

- not to be discriminated against in the provision of goods, facilities and services (except educational or transport facilities);

- not to be discriminated against in the provision of property or accommodation;

- to complain to an industrial tribunal about discrimination by employers or trade organisations;

- to proceed to the county court about discrimination in other areas.

(Law Society 1996)

The Disability Discrimination Act outlines the rights and responsibilities of disabled people and employers in a number of areas, including:

- recruitment and selection processes;

- the 'reasonable adjustments' employers must make to enable a disabled person to take up a job;

- terms and conditions;

- promotion, training and transfer opportunities;

- benefits and pension arrangements;

- harassment;

- retention and re-deployment.

However, people with learning difficulties will still need to obtain and be able to do a job before the Act applies. Employers will not have to appoint someone with a learning difficulty for a particular job, unless they want to. The Act will provide some protection for people who can prove they can do a job satisfactorily according to the job specification, and with the required adjustments by the employer, but who are rejected in favour of another candidate simply on the grounds of their physical impairments and/or learning difficulty.

> *"The Act is intended to remove the <u>additional</u> disadvantages which disabled people face when seeking employment. It does not require positive discrimination and does not oblige an employer to treat a disabled candidate <u>more favourably</u> than a candidate with no disability. If a disabled applicant, with reasonable adjustments, would still not be able to meet performance criteria reasonably regarded as essential to the tasks involved in the job then an employer can decline to make any such adjustments and can reject the person for the post" (Law Society 1996 p.22).*

However, the person affected will have to make a formal complaint about discrimination to an industrial tribunal and there are potentially many barriers to prevent people with learning difficulties from doing this. No legal aid is available for representation at industrial tribunals, although some advice agencies and voluntary organisations do offer this service. The individual concerned has to be prepared to go through this process and staff may not be experienced in supporting them in these situations.

Employment agencies involved in the research were unsure whether the Act would make employers more or less reluctant to give jobs to people with learning difficulties. Employers might prefer to keep people in the position of 'job placements' rather than take them on as employees, with the legal requirements and protections that now exist. However, there is little evidence so far about whether the Act will actually change the job situation for people with learning difficulties to any significant degree. Given that the problems people experience in jobs also closely relate to benefit issues, which the Act does not cover, the effect may be minimal. Nevertheless, the provisions in the Act are a basis, however limited, to challenging discrimination if and when it arises.

The Disability Discrimination Act: Key Points

- The Disability Discrimination Act says that disabled people, including people with learning difficulties, should not be discriminated against in relation to jobs, goods, services and facilities. However, it does not say that people should be treated more favourably than non disabled people.

- People who believe they have been discriminated against have to make an appeal to an industrial tribunal.

- Employment agencies are not sure whether the Act will help more people with learning difficulties get and keep jobs or not.

Summary – Employment

Wages are a potential source of income for people with learning difficulties. However, financial matters around work, particularly concerning benefit issues and their relationship to housing, are closely linked to whether people are likely to be offered work, able to accept it, or enabled to keep it. Related to this are issues around support, the control of money, expectations about appropriate spending, and prejudices about who can work. These matters are connected to the organisational, staff and family issues discussed in Chapters 3 and 4.

Specialist employment agencies in various parts of the country have been successful in promoting work opportunities for a whole range of people with learning difficulties, including those with greater support needs. However, changes to service contracts have affected the independence and flexibility of agencies in some areas.

The Disability Discrimination Act 1996 offers the potential for challenging exploitative working conditions and prejudice against people with learning difficulties in relation to jobs. It is unclear as yet whether this Act will be of great use to many people with learning difficulties but it is to be hoped that people will be supported in challenging discrimination under the Act where appropriate. However, to really affect work opportunities for people with learning difficulties, changes to the benefits system are also required.

Chapter

7

CONCLUSIONS - SUPPORTING CHANGE

There have been themes running throughout the preceding chapters, similar issues which crop up whether the focus is on work or benefits, practice or experience. This chapter brings these themes together to make conclusions about the personal money of people with learning difficulties. The perspective here is change: what needs to change, who needs to change, how might things change, so that the imbalance of power around people's money and their experiences of poverty can be addressed by individuals, organisations, national agencies and government alike. The framework of existing legislation and social policy restricts some options for change but there are many smaller, more local ideas which people can begin to think about and act upon. Many staff and organisations have already begun to look at issues around money and it is hoped that the conclusions and suggestions made here will support that process.

Supporting Change with People with Learning Difficulties

There is a long way to go before all people with learning difficulties have access to appropriate teaching, support and informal learning opportunities about money as essential and integral parts of personal development and life experience. Some have been denied information and experience to such an extent that a great deal of time and support is required to help them extend their access to, and control of, their own money. Approaches which build confidence, provide positive feedback and offer a range of learning experiences help people with learning difficulties develop their skills (Allen, Banks and Staite, 1991). Staff and families have key roles to play in this.

An example of this comes from the experience of Colin, a man with learning difficulties who now lives independently with a small amount of support from a keyworker. Colin lived for many years with his mother. He applied to the local council to be put on the housing list but when his mother died he was sent further forms from the housing department which he could not face, and so was eventually taken off the list. He then moved to a group home but he still had a dream of his own place, so eventually he re-applied to the housing department and was reinstated on the housing list. His keyworker helped him prepare for independent living while he was waiting for his own place:

> "I had a keyworker who helped me to prepare myself for independent [living]. I studied budgeting, cooking, housework, washing, form filling, and varied diet. At one point my keyworker took me shopping in a supermarket to demonstrate economical buying."

While he was waiting, Colin would occasionally spend time at a friend's flat while she was away. **"This helped me feel how it would be on my own"**, Colin said. Another experience he had which helped prepare him for managing by himself was with a social work student. The student worked with Colin in preparation for independent living and Colin was involved in her exams, as he describes below. This experience gave him confidence in the skills he had been learning and also persuaded the staff in his group home that he should be given more control over his own day-to-day life.

> "Students on placement were used to assist me and support with any problems arising. One of the students used my case for her exams. On this occasion I was given money out of petty cash. I had to buy bus tickets to town for us three, do my shopping, save enough for a coffee each and buy bus fares back. It was a bit nerve racking, because whether she passed or not depended on my confidence. Because I did so well, she passed. At my next review it was decided that I should be provided with money weekly to buy my own food and cook it, apart from Sunday lunch. I had to retain receipts for all expenditure. If I wasted it there was no back up...".

Eventually, Colin got his own flat and now manages his own financial affairs. He feels he has proved wrong all the people who thought he would never manage by himself.

> "Since I have been on my own I have organised my electricity by card, my gas stamps, and now by card, my telephone by a local trust and pay by stamps. My TV I pay by stamps, my insurance for contents I pay weekly. I am also a member of a club which I use to buy clothes etc. I use my local P.O. for paying my accounts, because they are very kind and helpful...
>
> A number of people felt that I would not succeed, but I have proved them wrong. I am happy and contented and the ones who looked on the black side have had to admit they were wrong."

The confidence, happiness and control over his own life which Colin has achieved are sometimes dismissed because they are not seen as relevant to the majority of people with learning difficulties, being seen as possible only for those with less severe impairments. However, as Colin says, there were people who doubted he could achieve the level of independence that he has; his potential was by no means appreciated by the people around him for much of his life. This experience is repeated time and time again in the examples described in this report, examples of people's lives changing in ways unthinkable to many around them. Mark's story demonstrates that even those with great support needs, who do not use speech and may have sensory impairments or additional physical impairments, and will always need help with personal tasks, can be empowered to have access to, and control of, their own money through the use of direct payments and innovative trust fund arrangements. Dorothy's experience suggests that what holds many people back is not essentially their physical impairments or learning difficulties but the attitudes of others and the opportunities available to them.

However, people do need careful and appropriate support. Michael's story shows how people can be abused financially and the deep effect this can have on their lives. Without skills and experience, people can be vulnerable to the commercial temptations and sales pitches we are all affected by. One research participant knew someone with learning difficulties who was persuaded to buy a satellite dish by a door-to-door salesman. He did not really know what a satellite dish was and, in fact, did not have a television.

Sometimes the way services are set up and funded creates a stark choice between the financial restrictions of residential or hostel living and the comparatively enormous financial demands of independent living. Some people lose their independent homes because they are not given enough appropriate support around finance but, as Esmin's story demonstrates (Chapter 6), practitioners are often placed in difficult positions in terms of knowing how to support people given the legislative restrictions of benefits. Poverty puts burdens on people with learning difficulties in the same way as it does other people, but the failure they can feel when independent living breaks down due to financial pressures is particularly severe. It represents the end of a dream which may have sustained them through many years of institutional or familial abuse; the return to even more restrictive living opportunities than they had before; and an enormous increase in the control others have over their lives.

> *"For most people with learning disabilities, the decision about where they live is governed by assumptions about the extent and type of personal assistance they require. If people leave supported accommodation in favour of employment, they may find themselves set adrift in impoverished circumstances, without the opportunity to return to settings which offer essential assistance. Layered onto this are unchallenged assumptions and fears about people's financial ineptitude, fecklessness, wasteful spending patterns and vulnerability to exploitation. Further, people with learning disabilities may find that difficulties surrounding money management may not be dealt with in a helpful or consistent fashion by support personnel. In turn, this may contribute to further reductions in people's access to and control of their money"* (Davis, Murray and Flynn, 1993 p. 25).

This report has given examples of thoughtful, patient and imaginative help given by staff to people about their money. An interesting example comes from a Scottish tenancy support team who did some specific work with a man in relation to a lump sum he had inherited. The man had never had £1,000 and could not really conceive of what this amount represented. When the support workers started asking him what he wanted to do with the money, they realised that he had no idea what a thousand pounds meant and so, rather than impose a prescriptive list of options, they spent time with the man going round shops and talking about what could be done with £1,000. Interestingly, they also recognised that the man might not have access to such an amount of money again or for a very long time. They therefore talked with the man over a period of time about his dreams and fantasies for his life, with a view to seeing if the money could help him achieve something he had only ever dreamed of.

It turned out the man had always dreamed of what it would feel like to just blow a lot of money all in one go. He dreamed of the feeling of having a pocket full of cash and of having no cares, no restrictions and no reprisals about what he did with the money. If he had just been given the money, then gone out and done this, he might well have been labelled as 'inept, feckless and wasteful', as Davis, Murray and Flynn put it, and not trusted with money in the future. However, the workers in this case recognised and validated this dream and agreed with the man that £200 of the money would be for him to 'blow' as he wanted and the rest used in other ways which he identified.

Second, they realised that the man's understanding of money was based on the concept of what could be done with £10, the only amount of money he had ever had access to in the past. He therefore requested the £200 in £10 notes and, with this pile of cash, went off to blow it. He did not have to account to anyone for what he did with the money and, to this day, what happened to the £200 remains his business. One hopes he had fun and satisfaction, whatever happened!

As Simons acknowledges (1995), staff have an important role to play in helping people use money from legacies in imaginative and empowering ways:

> *"I personally have known a number of people with learning difficulties who have been left legacies. In each case, the sum would have been enough either to buy a small property outright, or at least to provide a substantial deposit. However nobody (and in the past I would have to include myself here) ever suggested that they might try and use that capital. In at least two cases, the amount was sufficient to mean that the individual was no longer eligible for income support. As a result, they have ended up being charged directly for the services they use until their capital is reduced. In one case, a man is having to pay a considerable amount per week to live in a setting which he does not like and would not have chosen had any alternative been offered."* (Simons 1995 p.48)

Staff can help people with learning difficulties consider the possibility of making wills, giving them choice and control over who benefits from their money and possessions after their death. As noted in Chapter 2, people with learning difficulties are legally entitled to make a will if they are fully able to understand the legal agreement they are setting up (The Law Society and BMA 1996).

Supporting Change with People with Learning Difficulties: Key Points

- People might not have had the chance to develop key concepts and experiences about money.

- Some people will need an extensive period of time in which to learn about money.

- There are many examples of people achieving much more in terms of financial independence than anyone expected.

- Financial abuse or 'failure' can have a deep effect on people's lives. However, many non-disabled people hold unreasonable and incorrect assumptions about the financial ineptitude, fecklessness and vulnerability of people with learning difficulties.

> - Some people are presented with the stark choice of over-restrictive financial control in a residential/group home setting or no support at all in an independent setting.
>
> - Staff can have an enormous positive impact on people's lives if they are prepared to really get to know the people they work with, spending time to understand their concepts and their aspirations in relation to money and then helping them achieve as much of this as possible.
>
> - People should be encouraged to make a will where appropriate and possible. Staff can help people think about the imaginative use of legacies.

Supporting Change in Housing and Service Organisations

Changing practice and approach in relation to money matters needs to happen at various levels within housing and service organisations. Senior managers and directors are concerned about the increasing workload associated with dealing with appointeeship and receivership. The temptation is to create receivership units to deal with this but, as Chapter 4 discussed, this option can create restrictions for individual people with learning difficulties in relation to their money. Another option is to promote or support the creation of independent finance schemes in local areas. As the example in Chapter 5 describes, such schemes can go a long way towards meeting the need for a formal service, user-focused and independent of both service organisations and families. This example also shows that such schemes do not require much on-going funding; charges for the service cover expenses and are borne by the place where the individual lives.

The possibility of a much wider use of direct payments by people with learning difficulties following the implementation of the Community Care (Direct Payments) Act in 1997 presents local authorities with an alternative approach to giving people a much greater control over the money associated with their support services. Likewise, registration and inspection officers made suggestions to the research about the greater use of their powers to address personal money matters for people living in registered residential accommodation. Currently, inspectors can demand to see records of how residential care managers collect benefits and use rent allowances but can not demand to see records of how personal money is dealt with. Extending such powers would require further legislation but officers suggested that they should be aware of personal money matters, including appointeeship and receivership, in the registration and in the inspection process.

At a management level, organisations can help staff and people with learning difficulties work with money on a day-to-day basis with clear procedures for dealing with money, risk assessment and management policies, training and support for staff to reflect on their practice. Bradley and Manthorpe's work in this area, described in earlier chapters, indicates that staff benefit from an opportunity to talk through the dilemmas, conflicting approaches and experiences around money. For instance, one health trust which participated in the research suggested that practitioners can be helped in their work around money by a clear risk assessment and management policy. Such a policy creates a framework within which staff can, in conjunction with those they support, make decisions about the risks involved in any particular action. It challenges staff to become aware of their own approach to risk and how this might colour their perception of what risk is suitable for others to take. It provides a procedure for decision-making about risk and thus supports staff to take risks which they might otherwise feel too uncomfortable or unsure about.

Simons (1995) describes a number of barriers which prevent organisations, and the people within them, from changing practice or which make these changes very difficult. He notes that there is sometimes a resistance to change. The culture and management structures of service organisations are geared to maintaining traditional services, so that innovative practice is kept to the margins. Towell and Beardshaw (1991) list some of the factors necessary to promote 'ordinary life' principles in services for people with learning difficulties. They suggest that 'enabling authorities' are needed, which promote a shared vision for the services. Networks, strategies and clear management are also needed, along with a 'learning approach' to the work and individual planning (Dowson, 1991).

Supporting Change in Housing and Service Organisations: Key Points

- Changes to practices and approaches need to take place at all levels within organisations.

- Appointeeship and receivership should never be applied in a blanket fashion.

- A wider use of direct payments should be considered. People do not have to be able to manage their finances with little or no support to take advantage of a direct payment.

- There are possibilities for an expanded role for registration and inspection officers but it must be borne in mind that, under existing laws, registered residential care drastically restricts the personal benefits available to people with learning difficulties.

- Change in organisations can be supported by considering the formal procedures discussed in Chapter 5. Changing how organisations relate to people and their money affects the day-to-day context within which people work. Staff will vary in how they respond to such changes, some resisting them and some welcoming them. Discussion, training and support may well be necessary.

Supporting Change in Staff Practices and Approaches

In addition to considering formal structures and procedures which will clarify staff roles in relation to people's money and provide protective frameworks against abuse or its allegations, organisations can also support the development of professional practice. Changing ingrained ways of working is not an easy or quick process, as the manager of a community health trust described in Chapter 4 noted. This manager was attempting to change radically the whole way in which his organisation approached money matters at all levels. Through a programme of formal procedure, training, support and bringing in new staff from outside the organisation, the manager hoped to slowly change practice. Such wide-sweeping change requires a positive and supportive approach with staff, who need to feel valued, respected, involved and inspired about the changes.

Examples throughout this report show many small ways in which staff can work with people with learning difficulties, and their families where appropriate, to bring greater choice and control of personal money to the individual. For this approach to flourish, staff need to recognise the importance of money and its place in a rights framework, and be given the training, informal support and formal procedural back-up to address money matters.

Senior managers need to support staff by setting up systems and frameworks which encourage flexible, creative, human and person-centred approaches to supporting people with learning difficulties. Bradley and Manthorpe (1997; 1995) emphasise training and learning contexts which allow practitioners to discuss and debate the dilemmas and contradictions of their work in relation to real case stories.

> *"These scenarios were constructed to highlight the dilemmas faced by practitioners and to enable those currently working in care management to make connections between the histories and their own practice and personal experiences"* (Bradley and Manthorpe, 1997 p.75).

They describe the useful comments and the learning processes of social workers who attended workshops based on this approach. The case history approach highlighted the paucity of information and professional training about finance which many social workers have received. It also helped participants make links between client groups, and between their clients' experiences and their own experiences.

Bradley and Manthorpe show how the underlying values associated by practitioners with social work practice can cause conflict for them when they are forced to deal with the dilemmas presented by financial matters. For example, one research participant gave the example of a man whom staff were encouraging to do domestic tasks around the home, as a way of becoming more self-reliant and independent, but he chose instead to use some of his money to purchase domestic help privately so he would not have to do it. Staff in this organisation were torn between the view that the man could do what he liked with his money and the view that he should be encouraged to learn as many skills as possible for himself.

Staff development is integral to the development of creative, quality services. In addition to training, some research participants suggested that clear aims and a goal oriented approach by staff can help people with learning difficulties develop their skills and experience around money, and thus their potential for control of their money. As noted in previous chapters, many people with learning difficulties have been denied the most basic experiences around money and so staff should not assume that the people they support hold the same concepts and experiences about money as they do. For example, tenancy support workers in Scotland told the research about their work with one woman who needed a lot of support to manage in her own flat. The woman had lived in a long-stay hospital for many years and it took two years before she felt confident that her money was actually hers. It was only after these two years that the support workers could start to help her learn practical skills around budgeting and so on. During this time, the woman required substantial patient support to enable her to keep her home and the workers had continually to ask themselves how much, and in what ways, they could or should be involved in her money. Clearly, the time, cost and continuity of support necessary to help people learn about money are significant factors for services.

A key to this is really getting to know people with learning difficulties as individuals, not only in terms of their likes and dislikes, but as human beings with aspirations, dreams, hopes. It can be particularly difficult for individual staff to promote this approach to their work in the face of rigid and institutional organisational practices, and colleagues who abide by such systems. Nevertheless, there are small day-to-day ways, in individual contact with someone with learning difficulties, through which staff can help people have more access to, and control of, their money.

One way in which staff can help people with learning difficulties develop more control over their money is by actively promoting wider social networks for individuals. It is often through these networks that people meet friends, neighbours and others who can help them develop skills and opportunities associated with money.

Supporting Change in Staff Practices and Approaches: Key Points

- A new approach to working with people around money matters needs to be promoted in organisations which emphasises a flexible, creative, human and person-centred framework around money.

- Dealing with money should be firmly placed within an 'ordinary life' framework.

- Individual staff can think how they might apply such a framework in their day-to-day contact with people with learning difficulties, even if their organisation and colleagues operate in a more rigid and institutionalised way.

- Staff need management support, the opportunity to discuss dilemmas and also training to work within such an approach.

Supporting Change with Families

People's money can be controlled by families for a number of reasons (see Chapters 3 and 6), sometimes in their own interests but more usually out of concern and care for their relative. The responsibilities of appointeeship and receivership are taken seriously by many family members. Trust funds are seen as one of the few ways in which money can be passed to relatives which takes account of mental incapacity legislation and benefit regulations. Some families are part of innovative trust funds and circles of support around their relatives which bring access and control of money much closer to the person with learning difficulties. Others struggle to get their relatives the financial options available to most people, often with little support. One elderly mother of two sons with learning difficulties described her experience, noted in Chapter 2, in trying to set up a bank account in the name of one of her children:

"I am 82 year old and still caring for my two handicapped sons. I am appointee for one of my sons. It is a big responsibility for me now. I worry what he will do when I am gone. I took him to five banks before I could get him a book. I wrote to one bank and asked them to give me a reason why he could not have one. He said he did not have to give a reason. After an interview with the manager, he was given one. If I had been on the street begging, I could not have felt worse."

Many research participants also recognised that families need more information and guidance about the responsibilities and limits around their relative's money, especially in regard to appointeeship, receivership and trusteeship. The research heard of many situations in which families over-protect their relatives and, although understandable, this nevertheless restricts the rights and opportunities of people with learning difficulties.

Service and housing organisations must also work with families if people with learning difficulties are to be enabled to have more access to, and control of, their money. Chapter 3 looked at some of the difficulties parents and families face in respect to their relative's money.

"What parents do have in common is a genuine concern for their sons and daughters and a wish to play some part in determining what is provided for them. We can not stress enough the need for sensitive partnerships with parents from the start." (Mental Health Foundation 1996 p.99)

However, sometimes staff find themselves directly in conflict with families, as in Dorothy's example, or caught between the needs of families and the person with learning difficulties. Bradley and Manthorpe (1997) give a detailed example of the difficulties presented around finance for social workers whose client is the person with learning difficulties (who, in their example, was learning to have more control over his money but, as a result, had chosen not to pay the charges for his services) but who recognise and sympathise with the bewilderment and adjustments families have to make to their habitual ways of relating to their relative.

Changes in Banking

Banking is changing all the time. Will people with learning difficulties take part in these changes? Will the changes help or hinder people with learning difficulties gaining more control of their money?

Some research participants thought that the increasing use of 'plastic', rather than cash, could be a problem for some people with learning difficulties who have not been given many opportunities to experience the practicalities and concepts around money. If financial exchanges become more and more abstract with the use of direct debits, credit cards and so on, there is an argument that people with learning difficulties will be even more removed from understanding and controlling their spending.

On the other hand, other research participants thought that banking developments would increase the potential for involvement by people with learning difficulties in their financial situation. Telephone banking might enable people who can not write or can not physically get to a bank to implement decisions about their money personally. Banks are developing voice recognition systems that will enable people to use facilities at banks and over the telephone. Again, this could enable people with learning difficulties to have greater access to their account(s) but might not overcome barriers presented by banks around the non-disclosure of PIN numbers. Direct debits are already used quite widely by people with learning difficulties, to ensure regular payments without having to remember what has been paid and when. They can be helpful for those who have difficulties with budgeting.

Another banking development currently being piloted by the National Westminster Bank, with possible public use within the next two or three years, is a system which uses a plastic card instead of cash to buy things. This is not the same as a credit card, as the idea is to replace the exchange of cash. Cards will be 'charged' with a cash amount at a bank and then used for all purchases, even buying a newspaper at a corner shop or paying for a bus fare. Whether this makes the concepts and use of money more or less accessible to people with learning difficulties remains to be seen.

Banks and building societies are opening these sorts of accounts for their customers and thus should take the responsibility for finding a way round this situation in the payout rules that they design.

Legal Change Relating to Mental Incapacity

The Law Commission for England and Wales undertook a five year inquiry into the adequacy of legislation about mental capacity/incapacity and published its findings and recommendations for change in 1995 (HMSO 1995). Overall, the Law Commission proposes a major change to the law around mental incapacity. It proposes bringing together all the pieces of law about incapacity which have developed over the years, so that the law can be more coherent and comprehensive. It also recommends wide-ranging changes to the way in which judgements about incapacity are made and the practices of bodies such as the Court of Protection which become involved when someone is judged as being incapable of managing some part of their affairs.

The Law Commission recommends that mental incapacity should be judged solely on whether someone has understood the decision-making process in relation to a particular decision. It has proposed a new definition of mental incapacity which should be applied to each particular decision, at each particular moment in time, according to the facts of the decision. This is a 'functional' approach to making a judgement about capacity which considers the individual's ability to make a particular decision, at a particular moment in time, _after_ understanding relevant information presented in broad and simple language, and _after_ every possible step has been taken to enable the individual to participate in the decision-making. This approach should take into account specific issues around communication, for example if someone does not use speech or can not read or uses sign language, for example.

There are various bases upon which people are given the right in law to make decisions for someone else. The Law Commission proposes that when someone is given this right because of an individual's incapacity, then decisions should be made for the individual solely based on what constitutes their 'best interests'. At the moment this perspective is not actually enshrined in law, although it is seen as good practice.

The Law Commission suggests that this 'best interest' should be made with regard to the individual's past and present wishes and feelings. The individual should be encouraged to take part in the decision-making as fully as possible and efforts made to improve their ability to do so. Relevant consultation with others might be appropriate but this should not be a substitute for helping the individual to be as directly and fully involved as possible. Finally, a 'best interests' decision should be the *least* restrictive option available which will achieve the decision/action. It is important to consider what is appropriate for each individual and not apply a blanket approach (Letts 1992).

The Scottish Law Commission has recently published its recommendations for change to Scottish law about mental capacity. No law reform commission exists for Northern Ireland and it is unclear as yet whether changes to law affecting England and Wales will be applied to Northern Irish law as well.

Legal Change Relating to Mental Incapacity: Key Points

- The Law Commission's proposals for legal change aim to create a comprehensive and cohesive framework within which judgements can be made about someone's capacity to manage their financial, and other, affairs.

- The Law Commission proposes that these judgements are made in relation to a particular issue at a particular time. Judgements should be made after people have been given all the relevant information they need, in an accessible way, and after every possible step has been taken to enable them to take part in the decision-making.

- The least restrictive course of intervention in someone's affairs should always be tried first.

Changes to the Court of Protection and Receivership

Chapter 2 lists many of the current limitations and problems with the receivership system and examples have been cited throughout this report which demonstrate some of these problems. The Law Commission has made suggestions for changes to the Court of Protection which would address some of these problems. It is proposed that the existing Court of Protection be abolished and replaced by a new superior court of record, to separate it from its historical purpose and bring it under the modern legal system. Rather than being based solely in London, with no direct contact with the majority of its 'patients', the Law Commission suggests that the Court should move around the country and should cover all issues including personal and health matters, not just financial and property affairs.

The Law Commission proposes that in most cases the Court should give permission for someone to apply to be a receiver. Before an application is accepted, the Court should check the circumstances and background of the applicants, their reasons for application, how they might personally gain from the receivership and conduct a police check for convictions of fraud. If there are other ways of achieving the financial benefit for the individual rather than bringing them under the Court of Protection, then this option of lesser control should be chosen. The Law Commission proposes that the individual should be informed of the application on their behalf and their wishes sought about this.

These suggested changes would bring the individual concerned towards the centre of the process and provide a check for potential abuse of the system by applicants. It seems unclear how these proposals might affect independent financial or advocacy schemes and local authority 'receivership units'. The proposal for the Court of Protection to support the least restrictive option in dealing with people's money, and to encourage people to be as involved in their financial affairs as possible, might help people with learning difficulties maintain more control over their money even when they are not able to manage it all by themselves. Despite these proposed changes, service organisations and independent finance schemes still need to consider whether receivership is an appropriate way of enabling someone to have more access to, and control of, their money.

Changes to the Court of Protection and Receivership: Key Points

- The Law Commission proposes that the present Court of Protection be abolished and a new court set up within the court system, rather than part of the Lord Chancellors department.

- A much more rigorous approach to vetting potential receivers should be in place and, by travelling throughout the country, the new Court should have the opportunity to meet those whose assets it might take over.

- The Law Commission propose that the least restrictive option about controlling someone's money should apply, within the context of the proposals for changes to making judgements about mental incapacity.

- Organisations and independent finance schemes should still consider whether it is appropriate to apply for receivership from the Court of Protection, whether there are legal changes or not. Blanket approaches to receivership should not be used.

Changes to Benefits and Appointeeship

Research participants had suggestions about how the Department of Social Security could improve the appointee system. They suggested that more than one officer should interview potential appointees; there should be vetting of potential appointees with police checks for fraud; appointees should produce references; and there should be a rigorous and enforced system of reporting and monitoring the use of people's money by appointees.

Similar suggestions are made by Davis, Murray and Flynn (1993) in their study of the financial circumstances of people with learning difficulties. They recommend changes to the appointee system including training about learning difficulties for benefits adjudicators; more involvement by people with learning difficulties in appointee processes; and the development of quality assurance standards within the Benefits Agency, including better dissemination of information.

The Mental Health Foundation, in a recent major review of housing and services for people with learning difficulties, also propose changes to the benefits system. These include raising the value of the income support earnings disregard; allowing people with a severe learning difficulty to return immediately to incapacity benefits when they lose paid employment; raising severe disablement allowance to the level of incapacity benefit; extending the job seekers allowance work concessions to people who have long-term incapacity; and raising the weekly allowance paid to people in NHS homes to the same level as that paid to people in other residential homes (1996 p.82).

The Department of Social Security is responding to some of these criticisms by producing better guidance for potential appointees, which explains their duties in more detail, but this does not alter the fact that thousands of people with learning difficulties have their money controlled by people who are not checked, monitored or asked to show how the money is spent. The Benefits Agency also needs to respond much more efficiently to complaints of abuse and people with learning difficulties should be involved in the process of checking and monitoring such complaints.

In the light of all these potential difficulties with the appointee system, the Law Commission (1993) originally proposed that the Benefits Agency reviews appointeeships every six or twelve months, requiring the appointee to provide an account of how someone's money has been spent (Langan and Means 1996 p.297). However, this proposal was dropped following consultation and replaced with the suggestion that appointees be sent an annual inquiry which they complete and send back to the Benefits Agency. A further suggestion was made that appointeeships should be set up for a term of three to five years, after which the appointee would have to reapply (Law Commission 1995 p.58). Langan and Means' study recommended that more information and guidance be provided for appointees.

In addition to a governmental review of benefits, particularly in relation to the restrictions current benefits place on work opportunities, the Department of Social Security also need to look at the guidance, training and support it gives benefits officers about appointeeship. Complaints and monitoring procedures need to be established. As with the Court of Protection, the Department of Social Security also needs to develop more individually-based and time-specific judgements about mental capacity to prevent the label 'learning difficulty' being used as blanket 'proof' that someone can not manage their financial affairs.

Changes to Benefits and Appointeeship: Key Points

- Benefits may need to change to enable more people with learning difficulties to get and keep jobs. The use of disability working allowance should be considered for more people.

- The Department of Social Security should tighten up the appointee system, in line with Law Commission proposals. There needs to be a more rigorous vetting of applicants for appointeeship, a more thorough response to complaints and more monitoring of appointees.

Summary Conclusions - Supporting Change

The conclusion to be drawn from this research has to be that many people with learning difficulties are poor, many being denied as full an access to, and control of, their money as possible. This poverty needs to be seen within a wider disability and rights framework that links the experiences of people with learning difficulties with those of other disabled people and poor people. This report has told the stories of many people with learning difficulties about how their lives are restricted or controlled unnecessarily by the inappropriate control, and over-protection, of their money. Being poor restricts people's choices and opportunities. For people with learning difficulties, choices and opportunities are restricted in quite practical, day-to-day ways, as well as in wider legal contexts. Many stories in this report demonstrate that people with learning difficulties are being denied access to, and control of, their own money, to whatever extent they are able, on a very wide scale.

A rights framework is important because it clarifies an underlying value base for work with people around money matters. Although there are many practical dilemmas about how to support someone in relation to their money, the extent of someone's impairments or their need for support should not be the first criterion used to decide whether someone can be involved in their money or not. As Mark's story has illustrated throughout this report, a rights framework enables creative ways to be found which put the individual, even those with substantial support needs, at the centre of choice and opportunity about their money.

Hopefully, the situation is changing. The funding for this project, the interest in the research from participants from many organisations and contexts all over the UK, the challenging discussion of the issues presented here, the development of procedures, an increase in published work and the attempt to set up new schemes all indicate that people are beginning to recognise the importance of personal money matters and the need for change in this area. Many families, staff and organisations recognise the need for such change but just feel stuck about how to move forward, balancing protection and support with freedom and choice. As this report has acknowledged, there are no simple blueprints for how to achieve this balance. A starting point is a rights framework and the development of creative, flexible, person-centred support. Such support requires an organisational culture which encourages debate about values around money, an investigation of creative possibilities, an investment in learning, an embracing of personal change and a commitment to the least restrictive option for each person. Individual staff have a very important role to play in all of this and can be influential in enabling real change in people's lives but, to support this, organisations also need to invest in staff development.

The Preface described some of the experiences of Dorothy, Michael, Josie, Alan, Tom and Mark in relation to their money. As the Preface said, all these stories are true; they are not embroidered or over-emphasised for the sake of rhetoric. The stories are not unusual. People with learning difficulties face the same stark realities about money as other people. Their real experiences and opinions should inspire discussion and action around money issues. Money matters, it is part of life, part of choice and opportunity. Issues of rights, personal growth, an 'ordinary life', can not be really addressed without recognising the importance of money matters.

There is much that needs to be done, at national, local and individual levels. The recommendations which follow in the next chapter summarise VIA's suggestions for action in the light of this research.

Chapter

8

SUMMARY AND RECOMMENDATIONS

This report has covered a wide range of issues about people with learning difficulties and their money. Many of these issues are complex: legally, organisationally and personally. It is to be hoped that this report, and the research upon which it is based, contribute to vigorous debate and practical change at national, local and individual levels. Not all the issues have been covered here, or in as much detail as they might need. Practical answers are not always easy or obvious. So this report and these recommendations are a beginning.

This final chapter brings together Values Into Action's recommendations for action arising from the *Unnecessary Poverty Project*. Chapter 7 discussed the need for change in more detail. This chapter lists recommendations under headings, grouped thematically for convenience and clarity.

Chapter Contents:
- Recommendations For National Agencies And Legal Change
- Recommendations For Service Organisations And Paid Staff
- Recommendations For Independent Schemes
- Recommendations For Individuals And Families

General Recommendations

1. Personal money matters for people with learning difficulties should be understood within poverty and disability frameworks. Efforts should be made to link the issues and experiences related to people with learning difficulties with those of other poor people and poor communities, especially other disabled people.

2. People with learning difficulties should be recognised as, on the whole, poor people, by reason of low income and restricted opportunity and also because of restricted access to and control of their money.

Recommendations For National Agencies And Legal Change

The Law and Mental Incapacity

1. The government should introduce legislative changes to the law around mental incapacity. Judgements about mental incapacity should be made in relation to specific decisions, with appropriate information available, and according to someone's understanding of the decision-making process not the wisdom of their decision. The least restrictive option should be implemented when deciding someone is incapable of managing all or part of their financial affairs.

2. The label learning difficulties should never be used by itself as proof of mental incapacity. People's abilities and potentials should be judged in individual circumstances.

3. Solicitors should receive better guidance and information about frameworks and principles of work with people with learning difficulties.

The Court of Protection

1. Receivership should never be implemented as a blanket approach to all people with learning difficulties with financial assets over £5,000.

2. The Court of Protection should have greater contact with the individual person with learning difficulties, including a better opportunity for people to challenge and reverse receivership. A more stringent vetting of prospective receivers should be introduced. There should be more guidance for receivers about their duties.

3. Court of Protection officers should receive some training in issues around people with learning difficulties, their money and current approaches to supporting people.

4. The government should introduce legislation in line with the Law Commission's recommendations about changes to the Court of Protection.

Trust Funds

1. Trustees need better guidance about setting up trust deeds so that they can be aware of the principles, remit and possibilities of trust funds. Trust deeds should allow the possibility of change in the person with learning difficulties' circumstances.
2. A trust fund should have three or four trustees, all of whom are actively involved in the individual's life. The individual should be involved in the decisions of the trust fund. An independent advocate can support this process.
3. Trust funds should be encouraged to use legacies and capital creatively and take on direct payments where appropriate.
4. Solicitors should receive more guidance and training about involvement in innovative trust funds relating to people with learning difficulties.

Wills

1. People with learning difficulties should be encouraged to make wills where possible.

The DSS and Social Security Benefits

1. The DSS should provide more training, guidance and information for its officers in dealing with people with learning difficulties, particularly in relation to appointeeship.
2. DSS officers should be much more aware of the potential abuse of appointeeships.
3. Benefit changes are needed to encourage and enable more people with learning difficulties to take up and keep jobs. The income disregard should be raised and a sliding scale of benefits introduced.
4. Housing benefit regulations should not discriminate against disabled people who need personal live-in assistance to live independently.
5. The need for an appointee should be questioned by DSS officers. Prospective appointees should be more carefully vetted and monitored. Appointeeships should be for a fixed term.

6. The DSS should review the process for dealing with complaints about appointees.

Banking

1. People with learning difficulties, along with other disabled people, should be included by banks and building societies when drawing up policies and procedures. The fact that someone needs support to operate an account should not be used as proof of them being incapable of operating an account.

2. Banks and building societies should provide clearer guidance to branch managers and staff about the possibilities for people with learning difficulties to use accounts.

3. Inability to sign a name, or the label learning difficulties, should not be used as a sole reason for refusing to open an account.

Employment

1. Legislation is needed to introduce benefit changes which will enable more people with learning difficulties to find and keep jobs (see above).

2. Staff should be aware of the Disability Discrimination Act and be prepared to support people, or find them the advice they need, to challenge discrimination.

3. People with learning difficulties should not be prevented from taking up job opportunities because of the consequent change or risk to their benefit income.

Recommendations For Service Organisations And Paid Staff

Service Organisations

1. Organisations should provide training for staff around money matters. They should provide opportunities and an organisational climate in which staff can discuss dilemmas, values and choices.

2. Access to, and control of, personal money should be kept as close to the individual as possible. This includes the control of benefit and bank books where at all possible.

3. Receivership and appointeeship should never be used in a blanket fashion and should be avoided if at all possible because they take control away from the individual.

4. It should be assumed that people are able to manage all or part of their money, until there is substantial proof to the contrary.

5. Organisations should develop risk assessment and management policies and procedures for prevention/dealing with financial abuse. Procedures should be placed within a clear value base and staff trained in their use.

6. People with learning difficulties should have bank, building society and post office accounts in their own name. Hospital banks should not be used for people living in the community.

7. The opportunities offered by legacies and direct payments should be investigated creatively. High support needs should not be an used as a reason for refusing direct payments.

8. The balance of protection against freedom to take risks, make mistakes and make 'unwise' decisions about money should be thoroughly addressed. Managers should help staff think through these dilemmas.

9. Managers should be aware of the financial consequences for people with learning difficulties if they are placed in registered residential housing.

10. Registration and inspection officers should investigate the possibility of extending their role to consider how homes assist people to manage their personal money. Legislation will be required to give this role legal standing.

Staff Practices

1. Staff should be trained and supported in working within flexible, person-centred, creative, rights-based frameworks. Staff should get to know the people they work with individually, especially about their likes and dislikes, hopes, dreams and aspirations. Staff should be encouraged to work creatively with people around money matters. They should be supported by risk assessment policies.

2. Staff need some training in the legal and national context of money and how to challenge the inappropriate use of the legal options available.

3. Staff need a supportive environment within which to discuss their own dilemmas, experiences, values and approaches to working with people's money.

4. Control of money should not be used to control behaviour.

5. Staff should be prepared to work with families in relation to people's money. They should also be prepared, where necessary, to challenge abuse or inappropriate control of money by families.

Recommendations For Independent Schemes

Independent Schemes and Advocacy

1. The role of independent advocacy, as a scheme or in individual cases, should be considered much more widely in relation to people's money.

2. Independent money schemes must be truly independent. Their client should be the person with learning difficulties. They should be prepared to advocate on behalf of that person where necessary.

3. The person with learning difficulties should have a choice as to whether they are part of such a scheme. Other options may be possible. People should be able to leave a scheme if they want to.

4. Independent schemes should be cautious about the automatic use of appointeeship or receivership. Blanket procedures should never be implemented.

5. Independent schemes should be careful about institutionalising control and choices about money. Individual scheme users should still control the use of their money and be able to decide what happens to it.

Recommendations For Individuals And Families

Families

1. Families may need the support of organisations in terms of allowing relatives to have more access to and control of their money. They may also need support to change their attitudes and approaches to their relative's money, which may well be part of the family patterns. Families need support to realise that their relative may have different aspirations and opportunities than they envisaged.

2. Families need to feel that the organisation is skilled and trust-worthy in how it deals with their relative's money.

3. Relatives need more guidance about the roles of appointee, receiver and trustee.

4. Families must never assume that their relative's money automatically belongs to the family. Unnecessary restrictions on their relative's development should not be enforced merely to maintain the financial status quo.

Education and Learning

1. People with learning difficulties should be given the opportunities and support they need to learn about money. It should be recognised that this might take a lot of time and involve risk and mistakes.

2. Staff must know the individual, their concepts about money and their hopes and dreams, for effective learning to be supported.

3. There is a balance between risk and protection: organisations, staff and families should not necessarily put protection first. Good risk assessment procedures help this process.

4. Staff should help individuals claim all the benefits to which they are entitled.

5. People with learning difficulties may need debt and other financial advice.

6. People may need victim support when they experience financial abuse or crime against them. An experience of financial abuse, by itself, should not be seen as proof of incapacity to manage money.

Appendix

1

THE RESEARCH

This report is based upon research undertaken for the *Unnecessary Poverty Project* at Values Into Action between June 1996 and May 1997. The *Unnecessary Poverty Project* was funded by the National Lottery Charities Board. The project team consisted of Catherine Bewley, researcher; Andrew Holman, project manager; and Jean Collins, director of VIA.

The initial perspective for the project was that many thousands of pounds are paid out in benefits and service costs on behalf of people with learning difficulties and yet many people are extremely poor in terms of the actual money which they have access to and control of. Money is part of life; it is intimately tied to choice and empowerment. This project aimed to find out how and why people with learning difficulties are denied access to, and control of, their own money.

The project therefore looked at a range of situations in which people with learning difficulties live (hospital, group homes, residential homes, independent accommodation, with families) from the perspectives of organisational procedures and inter-personal dynamics. Issues relating to the legal interventions which can be made around someone's money, employment issues, education and learning issues were also investigated. Through a variety of publications and networks, individuals and organisations throughout the UK were contacted directly or invited to participate in the research. The researcher travelled around the UK, meeting and interviewing people. Information was also gathered by telephone interviews and via letters.

A total of 170 people took part in this research. Forty five people with learning difficulties took part directly in the research; the stories of others were told by supporters and advocates. Another 65 participants were practitioners and support staff; 30 were senior managers and finance staff; 10 were advocates and advisors for self advocacy groups; 5 were parents; 10 were representatives from national voluntary organisations; 5 were representatives from national legal or government agencies dealing with people's money. On the next page is a table with a more detailed breakdown of the main categories of participants.

People who attended the following events contributed views and experiences to the research: the Norah Fry workshop in Bristol (November 1996); VIA's Housing Participation conference (October 1996); VIA's annual conference (November 1996); and VIA's Funding Freedom conference (March 1997).

The following table breaks down the main categories of participants from major organisations but does not include all national-level participants, all individuals or those who were contacted though the workshops and conferences listed above.

PARTICI-PANTS	Senior Managers	Finance Staff	Service Managers	Social Workers & Support Staff	Other Paid Staff	People with Learning Difficulties	TOTALS
Hospital & Commun/y Health Trusts	2	1	3	1			7
Local Authorities	4	1	4	9	2	8	28
Housing Assoc/tions	2	2	2	1		2	9
Voluntary Sector Providers	1	1		3	1	4	10
Indepen/t. Finance Schemes	1						1
General Voluntary Groups					10	1	11
Employ/t. Schemes				7		1	8
Adult Education Groups					1	6	7
Citizen Advocacy Groups					4		4
Self Advocacy Groups					6	22	28
TOTALS	10	5	9	21	24	45	114

Appendix
2

REFERENCES

Age Concern, MENCAP, Mind, NAHAT and the Disabled Living Foundation, (1992). *Other people's money: guidance on the responsibilities of formal carers in the NHS*. London, Age Concern England.

Aspis, S. (undated). *Laws about our rights*. London, People First.

Atkinson, D. (1989). *Someone to turn to: the social worker's role and the role of front line staff in relation to people with mental handicaps*. Kidderminster, British Institute of Mental Handicap.

Balloch, S. and Robertson, G. (1995). *Charging for social care*. London, National Institute of Social Work.

Beresford, P. (1996). Poverty and disabled people: challenging dominant debates and policies. *Disability and Society*, 11(4), 553-568.

BMA and Law Society (1995). *Assessment of mental capacity: guidance for doctors and lawyers*. London, British Medical Association.

Bradley, G. and Manthorpe, J. (1997). *Dilemmas of financial assessment: a practitioner's guide*. Birmingham, Venture Press.

Bradley, G. and Manthorpe, J. (1997). The price of care: charging for services for people with learning disabilities. *Journal of Learning Disabilities for Nursing, Health and Social Care*, 1(2).

Bradley, G. and Manthorpe, J. (1995). The dilemmas of financial assessment: professional and ethical difficulties. *Practice*, 7(4), 21-30.

Brown, H. and Stein, J. (1997). *Implementing adult protection policies*. Milton Keynes, The Open University.

Brown, H. and Benson, S. (1992). *A practical guide to working with people with learning disabilities: a handbook for care assistants and support workers*. London, Hawker Publications.

Carson, D. (ed.) (1987). *Making the most of the Court of Protection: a guide to the law relating to the Court of Protection: on making use of the Court's services*. London, King's Fund.

Centre for Policy on Ageing, (1996). *A better home life*. London, CPA.

Child Poverty Action Group (1996). *Welfare benefits handbook*. London, CPAG.

Curran, C. and Grimshaw, C. (1996). Mental Health Act notes: the Court of Protection and management of property and affairs of patients. *Psychiatric Care*, 3(1), 33-36.

Davis, A., Murray, J. and Flynn, M. (1993). *Normal lives? The financial circumstances of people with learning disabilities*. Manchester, NDT.

Department of Health, 1997. *Community Care (Direct Payments) Act 1997. Policy and practice guidance*. London, HMSO.

Disability Alliance (21st ed.) (1996). *Disability rights handbook*. London, Disability Alliance Education & Research Association.

Dowson, S. (1991). *Moving to the dance: or service culture and community care*. London, VIA.

Dunning, A. (1995). *Citizen advocacy with older people: a code of good practice*. London, Centre for Policy on Ageing.

Grant, L. (1995). *Disability and debt: the experience of disabled people in debt*. York, Joseph Rowntree Foundation.

Greenwich Social Services, (1993). *Recognising and responding to the abuse of adults with learning disabilities*. London, Greenwich SSD.

Holman, A. and Collins, J. (1997). *Funding freedom*. London, Values Into Action.

Holman, A. (1997). Broken promises: housing benefit changes. Part 2. *Community Living*, January.

Holman, A. (1996). Broken promises: housing benefit changes. Part 1. *Community Living*, October.

Holman, A. (1995). *Independent living for people with learning difficulties: sample trust deed*. London, Values Into Action.

Hughes, A., McAuslane, L. and Schur, H. (1996). Comparing quality of life for people with learning disabilities and people who are unemployed or retired. *British Journal of Learning Disabilities*, 24, 99-103.

Jenkins, G. (1996). *Residents' money: a guide to good practice*. London, Age Concern England.

Kinsella, P. (1993). *Group homes. An ordinary life?* Manchester, National Development Team.

Lambeth Accord and Change, (1995). *This is how we want to live: quality standards and rights: people with learning disabilities in Lambeth speak out*. London, Lambeth Accord.

Langan, J. and Means, R. (1996). Financial management and elderly people with dementia in the UK: as much a question of confusion as abuse? *Ageing and Society*, 16, 287-314.

Langan, J. (forthcoming). In the best interests of elderly people? The role of local authorities in handling and safeguarding the personal finances of elderly people with dementia. *Journal of Social Welfare and Family Law*.

Law Commission, (1995). *Mental incapacity*, Law Com 231, London, HMSO.

Law Society, (1996). *Enduring powers of attorney: guidelines for solicitors*. London, The Law Society.

Law Society, (1996). *How to comply with the Disability Discrimination Act 1995*. London, The Law Society.

Letts, P. (1992). Their money in your hands? *Community Living*, April 1992, p.9.

Means, R. (1996). Handling other people's money. *Care Plan*, June, 24-27.

Means, R. and Langan, J. (1996). Money 'handling', financial abuse and elderly people with dementia: implications for welfare professionals. *Health and Social Care in the Community 4(6), 353-358.*

Means, R. and Langan, J. (1996). Charging and quasi-markets in community care: implications for elderly people with dementia. *Social Policy and Administration, 30(3), 244-262.*

MENCAP, (1996). *Throwing away the key: a MENCAP report on the proposals for changing entitlement to the mobility component of disability living allowance*. London, MENCAP.

MENCAP, (undated). *Leaving money by will to people with learning difficulties*. London, MENCAP.

Mental Health Foundation, (1996). *Building expectations: opportunities and services for people with a learning disability*. London, Mental Health Foundation.

Millar, S. (1996). 'Anger over thousands of disabled set to be losers in bonus share deal', *The Guardian*, 5/11.

Public Trust Office, (1995). *Information for nursing homes, hospitals and other carers*. London, Public Trust Office.

Public Trust Office, (undated). *Factsheet 5: applying for a direction of the public trustee.* Public Trust Office.

Quinn, A. (1995). *A guide to families wishing to make legal provision for a learning disabled member*. London, Anthony Quinn & Company.

Rowe, J., Davies, K.N., Baburaj, V. and Sinha, R.N. (1993). F.A.D.E. A.W.A.Y.: the financial affairs of dementing elders and who is the attorney? *Journal of Elder Abuse and Neglect*, 5(2), 73-79.

Simons, K. (1995). *My home, my life: innovative approaches to housing and support for people with learning difficulties*. London, Values Into Action.

Sinason, J. (1995). *Care in the community for young people with learning disabilities: the client's voice*. London, Jessica Kingsley.

Todd, M. and Gilbert, T. (1995). *Learning disabilities: practice issues in health settings*. London, Routledge.

Walsh, B. (undated). *Processes and procedures for establishing trusts and UCILS*. London, Disability Advocacy Network.

Wertheimer, A. (1991). *Making it happen: employment opportunities for people with severe learning difficulties*. London, King's Fund.

USEFUL ORGANISATIONS

Action on Elder Abuse
1268 London Road
London SW16 4ER
Tel: 0181 - 679 8000

Age Concern England
1268 London Road
London SW16 4ER
Tel: 0181 - 679 8000

Benefits Agency
PO Box 51
Heywood
Lancashire OL10 2GG
Tel: 015320 - 324000

Citizen Advocacy Information and Training
Unit 2K
Leroy House
436 Essex Road
London N1 3QP
Tel: 0171 - 359 8289

Court of Protection
Stewart House
24 Kingsway
London WC2B 6JX
Tel: 0171 - 269 7157/7358/7317

Department of Health and Social Services (Northern Ireland)
Dundonald House
Upper Newtownards Road
Belfast BT4 3SF
Tel: 01232 - 520000

Department of Social Security
The Adelphi
1-11 John Adam Street
London Wc2N 6HT
Tel: 0171 - 962 8000

Disability Action (Northern Ireland)
2 Annadale Avenue
Belfast BT7 3JR
Tel: 01232 - 491011

Disability Alliance Education & Research Association
Universal House
88-94 Wentworth Street
London E1 7SA
Tel: 0171 - 247 8776
Tel: 0171 - 247 8763 (rights advice line for disabled people & their advisors)

Enable
6th Floor
7 Buchanan Street
Glasgow G1 3HL
Tel: 0141 - 226 4541

High Court (Northern Ireland)
Royal Court of Justice
Chichester Street
Belfast BT1 3JU
Tel: 01232 - 235111

Law Commission (England and Wales)
Conquest House
37-38 John Street
Theobalds Road
London WC1N 2BQ
Tel: 0171 - 411 1220

Law Commission (Scotland)
140 Causewayside
Edinburgh EH9 1PR
Tel: 0131 - 668 2131

MENCAP
123 Golden Lane
London Ec1Y ORT
Tel: 0171 - 454 0454

National Association of Inspection and Registration Officers
28 Broom Lane
Rotherham SE60 3EL
Tel: 01709 - 366237

Northern Ireland Council for Voluntary Action
127 Ormeau Road
Belfast BT7 1SH
Tel: 01232 - 321224

Office of Care and Protection (Northern Ireland)
Royal Court of Justice
PO Box 410
Chichester Street
Belfast BT1 3JF
Tel: 01232 - 235111

People First
Instrument House
207-215 Kings Cross Road
London Wc1X 9DB
Tel: 0171 - 713 6400

Scottish Council for Voluntary Organisations
18-19 Claremont Crescent
Edinburgh EH7 4QD
Tel: 0131 - 556 3882

Standard Conference on Citizen Advocacy for Wales
c/o Montgomeryshire Citizen Advocacy Project
Office 1, The Courtyard
Severn Street
Newtown
Powys SY16 2AQ
Tel: 01686 - 629951

117

Values Into Action
Oxford House
Derbyshire Street
London E2 6HG
Tel: 0171 - 729 5436

Wales Council for Voluntary Action
Llys Ifor
Crescent Road
Caerphilly
Mid Glamorgan CF8 1XL
Tel: 01222 - 869224

Appendix

4

<u>GLOSSARY</u>

Appointee
Someone who applies to the DSS to be the person to collect and use the benefits of a claimant who is incapable of doing this for themselves.

Benefits Agency
The agency of the DSS which deals with benefits claims and pays benefits.

Court of Protection
The office of the Supreme Court, based in London, which deals with the assets of people mentally incapable of managing their financial affairs.

Direct Payment
A payment made by a local authority to an individual in lieu of the services the individual has been assessed as needing.

Disability Living Allowance
A social security benefit paid by the DSS to people who are not able to work due to disability.

Disability Working Allowance
A social security benefit paid by the DSS to disabled people who work sixteen hours or less per week and earn £90 or less per week.

DSS (Department of Social Security)
The government department which oversees policy and practice around social security benefits. The DSS base at Longbenton in Newcastle-upon-Tyne is the national office which deals with disputes about appointeeship.

Incapacity Benefit
A social security benefit paid by the DSS to people who are incapable of working, according to medical evidence.

Income Disregard
The amount of money (currently £15) which people claiming income support can earn before their benefits are reduced.

Income Support
A social security benefit paid by the DSS to people who qualify by reason of low income, under certain rules about income and savings levels.

Law Commission
The Law Commissions of England/Wales and Scotland exist to consult on, and make recommendations about, legal changes to the law around mental incapacity.

Mental Incapacity
A legal and medical term defining a judgement that someone is not able to manage their affairs or make certain decisions by reason of mental disorder.

Mobility Allowance
Part of disability living allowance, paid to people who need assistance to get around. Now called mobility component.

Patient
A Court of Protection term referring to people covered by the Court's jurisdiction.

Personal Allowance
A DSS benefit paid directly to people who live in residential or nursing homes.

Practitioner
A trained professional working with people with learning difficulties, usually referring to a social worker.

Public Trust Office
An executive agency which provides administrative support for the Court of Protection, registers powers of attorney and administers some trust funds.

Receiver
Someone appointed by the Court of Protection to manage an individual's money and liaise with the Court on behalf of someone who comes under the Court's jurisdiction.

Service Manager
A paid professional working in a service organisation who manages paid staff working with people with learning difficulties.

Service Organisation
An organisation offering housing, support and/or health services.

Staff
In this report, staff refers to anyone paid to work with people with learning difficulties on a day-to-day basis, especially those working for service organisations.

Therapeutic Earnings
The amount of money people with mental incapacity are able to earn per week before their benefits are reduced (currently £45). Requires medical evidence of incapacity.

Trust Fund
A legal arrangement by which one or more people (trustees) manage someone's money and financial assets according to the terms of a trust deed.